THE STOP DRINKING EXPERT: ALCOHOL LIED TO ME UPDATED AND EXTENDED EDITION

Join me for a free quit drinking webinar at
www.stopdrinkingexpert.com

D1726527

Introduction

When I wrote the book 'Alcohol Lied To Me,' I had no idea the impact it would make to problem drinkers around the world. I certainly had no idea it would end up helping hundreds of thousands of people out of the miserable loop of alcoholism. I only wanted to document how I had finally dealt with my problem without any of the usual pain and struggle.

I had spent the prior decade feeling like an abject failure. No matter what I did, I could not seem to get back in control of my drinking. I felt broken, and it appeared that everyone I asked for help felt the same. My drinking aside, I was a successful professional man, with a beautiful family and plenty of evidence of my success. It appeared nobody was going to help me with my drinking unless I was prepared to stand up in front of a bunch of strangers and label myself a weak-willed alcoholic.

Alcohol Lied To Me is how I escaped the trap of functional alcoholism without any of those embarrassing group meetings, no dangerous medication, expensive rehab, or ineffective willpower. It has been a savior to so many successful, loving, caring, and amazing people whose only flaw is being in a loop with their drinking. It offers a compelling alternative solution to the twelve steps.

1. No need to label yourself an alcoholic
2. No religion or giving your problem to a higher power
3. A logical and intelligent approach to problem drinking
4. It's proven effective
5. The only Trustpilot 5-star rated quit drinking program

This book features all the best advice of 'Alcohol Lied To Me,' and the secrets I share with attendees of Quit Drinking Bootcamp. Plus all the great sober living tips I have picked up over a decade of helping problem drinkers around the world.

Before we go any further, congratulations on being here. A trite statement? I don't think so; the very act of reading these words should be seen as a powerfully positive action. It means you are not a part of the vast majority of problem drinkers who never do anything about this insidious drug. A drug that we don't even like to call a drug. Go into any local bar and ask the customer how their drug use is going, and you will get a mixture of abuse and ridicule in response.

The truth is, this social *Heiterkeit* pleasantry is a drug and a dangerous one at that. Alcohol kills millions of people every year, and yet we are repeatedly made to feel that if you refuse to join in with the consumption of attractively packaged poison, it's you who has a problem. In the western world, we live in a bubble of unreality around this drug. When you write down the nonsense, we believe about this drug; it looks quite insane.

- We toast our 'good health' with a liquid proven to cause seven significant forms of cancer.
- We drink when we feel down, even though alcohol is a depressant.
- Alcohol is used to help us with insomnia, even though we know it disturbs sleep.
- Drinkers are suspicious of the people who choose not to drink the poison, not the other way around.

We have got ourselves into a bizarre situation where we are looking at black and insisting it is white. It's is the unpicking of this universal distortion that explains why 'Quit Drinking Bootcamp' has been so useful for so many problem drinkers around the world. Attending Bootcamp is a bit like going to see Penn And Teller, the famous illusionists. First they wow you with a spectacular illusion and you can see no other explanation than to call it magic. However, then they come back on the stage and show you how the trick was performed. From this point on, you will never be able to be fooled by that illusion again.

It doesn't matter how long you live; you will never be able to label that routine as 'magic' again. Even if you reach the ripe old age of 100-years-old, that piece of theatre will fail to fool you again. At 'Quit Drinking Bootcamp' I show you how the alcohol trick is being performed. I show you why you believe that drinking helps you relax and cope with life. I reveal why you think that alcohol enables you to be more sociable and confident in public. I shine the spotlight of truth on all the nonsense and illusion of this drug. I proudly reveal myself to be the man who forever spoils alcohol for you, for good!

While it is true that you can go through this book, complete my online course, or come to Bootcamp and still go back to drinking after. However, it will not be the same. You will never be able to drink using the old excuses and justification you previously employed to explain your actions. That might sound insignificant, but it is deeper and more profound than you could imagine. Your beliefs are the secret to everything in your life, both good and bad.

I always ask drinkers why they drink, and often I get the answer 'for the buzz' or 'for the sensation of euphoria' that it brings to life. To which I ask, 'if that's what you want, why not use heroin'? After all, heroin is a much 'better' drug if that's what you are chasing. Of course, I am joking but only to make a point. The reason why problem drinkers don't feel the pull to use something more potent like heroin is that they believe it would be devastating to their life. They are right but more than that it demonstrates that their beliefs and subconscious programming are perfectly aligned around this drug. We just don't do things that we believe will be harmful to us. Ergo, if you still drink alcohol, it is because your beliefs around this drug are currently not correctly positioned. My goal is to get your beliefs around alcohol to match and mirror those you have about other (and less socially acceptable) dangerous drugs.

Sometimes at Bootcamp, I see a few furrowed brows at this point, and a few hands will go up seeking clarification. I will be told 'I know alcohol is destroying my life, that's why I am here.' However, it is crucial to understand that there is an enormous difference between your conscious beliefs and your subconscious beliefs. Almost everyone on planet earth consciously believes that their life would be better if they were rich. Sadly most of them also have subconscious beliefs that block such a utopia ever appearing. They have been programmed at an unconscious level since the day they were born. Taught to believe that money is the root of all evil, rich people are corrupt and immoral and so on.

There are two parts of our brain, but they are hugely unbalanced. The conscious mind is tiny and weak compared to the subconscious mind. It is for this reason alone that willpower nearly always fails when used against alcohol problems. Willpower resides in the conscious mind, but your drinking problem is not there - it is in the vastly more powerful subconscious part of your brain. If you have repeatedly failed to moderate your drinking in the past, don't feel bad. You are not weakwilled or any of the other negative labels we tend to apply. The reality is you have repeatedly been turning up to a gunfight with a knife.

This rule does not just apply to alcohol. It affects every aspect of our lives daily. If you consciously believe you would be happier if you weighed less and decide to go on a diet. However, at the same time, you have buried beliefs that dieting is a miserable and challenging ordeal. Guess what the long term result of your actions will be. This is the very reason why 95% of people who go on a weight loss diet will not only re-gain the lost weight but will add on average an extra 2-3 lbs on top.

Sticking your head outside the bubble of unreality is a beautiful thing to do. It signifies you are in a small but impressive group of people. Most people who are worried about their drinking never do anything about it... until it's too late. Be proud that you are not one of those people; you are openminded enough to consider that what you currently believe may not be serving you, may not even be true.

Your journey into the truth begins with a question. Why do you drink?

What is alcohol giving you? Take a few moments to write down what you currently believe the benefits of alcohol are. Common answers range from relaxation and drinking to ease social anxiety to pain man-agement and self-medication. Be honest with yourself and be specific. Stating you drink because you 'like it', is too vague. What specifically do you like, what pleasure is it moving you towards or what pain does it appear to push you away from?

www.stopdrinkingexpert.com

Fun, relaxation, socializing, self-confidence, a Kick

CHAPTER 1: DO YOU HAVE A PROBLEM WITH ALCOHOL?

Most people pick up this book wanting to know, 'Do I have a problem?' Some are hoping this book will allow them to conclude that they are doing nothing wrong and now conveniently have some written evidence to back up and endorse the continuation of their habit. Others are aware that they are no longer in control and want help to stop drinking and to stay quit. Stopping drinking, as we all know, is the easy bit. Staying permanently off the alcohol is the real problem.

So let's answer that initial burning question: Do you have a problem with alcohol?

Yes, but there is not actually anyone who drinks alcohol that doesn't have a problem. Alcohol is in itself a problem and not a solution (as many believe it to be). Therefore, if this substance is in your life in any form, you cannot help but have a problem. As you will discover in this book, alcohol is an addictive toxin packaged into attractive bottles, marketed with billions of dollars of advertising, and so deeply ingrained in popular culture that we can no longer see it for what it really is.

One thing you will quickly discover is that people get very upset when you criticize this drug; they don't even like you referring to it as a drug! Your alcohol-drinking friends would tell me to stop being so melodramatic. They will probably argue that many millions of people around the world manage to enjoy alcohol responsibly, and it doesn't negatively affect their lives in the slightest. Some might go further to suggest that for some the occasional drink improves or enhances their life. However, this counter-argument to my opening gambit only holds water if you suspend the reality that alcohol is actually a poison created from the by-product of decaying vegetable waste.

This book is all about opening your eyes to what is going on behind the smoke and mirrors of alcohol. In truth, alcohol is a poison (a registered poison no less)! So with that fact in mind, how can anyone argue that the habitual consumption of poison is a positive thing?

Many people find this concept tricky to accept initially because we are conditioned to see alcohol, not as a poison, but merely a harmless social pleasantry. So for the sake of argument, let's replace the poison used in this argument with a different toxin, hydrogen cyanide, for example. Imagine how illogical it would be to try and defend the consumption of cyanide!

Would you say that someone who only consumes cyanide infrequently was a social user of the chemical? Yet this is exactly what we do with alcohol. Of course, your first response to this will probably be an objection to the comparison. Many will complain that cyanide will kill you stone dead, whereas alcohol just makes you merry. It is true that neat cyanide will kill you, but then so will 100% pure alcohol. Heavily diluted cyanide won't kill you, but it will make you very ill. Are we really a million miles away as comparisons go?

Once you become aware that the emperor isn't actually wearing any clothes, and realize that alcohol is none of the things the marketing suggests it is, only then can you start to deconstruct some of the popular language surrounding its use. We talk of these 'normal' and 'social drinkers,' the people who can consume alcohol at parties and social occasions but don't appear to be dependent on it to remain functional. Of course, even the most hardened alcoholic at some point was what we would describe as a 'social drinker.' Before the mousetrap of alcoholism snapped closed on them, they were considered just as normal as the next guy. The poor problem drinkers looked at them and wondered why they couldn't drink for fun, just like them.

And so the cycle of addiction continues. Social drinkers slowly become alcohol-dependent problem drinkers, and instantly in the eyes of society, they stop being 'normal' and become weak-willed, pitifully sad people who, for some reason, can't consume an addictive toxin and stay in control of it. Alcohol is many things, but it is certainly not the life-enhancing, glitzy elixir that the advertising agencies would have us believe or that generations have passed down in collectively endorsed lies.

We believe that alcohol makes a party go with a swing, and yet the next day, we happily use words of destruction to describe what a great time we had. We stare out from bloodshot eyes, with a tongue feeling like a butcher's chopping block, and gleefully report that last night we were "slaughtered" or any one of a hundred other different terrible adjectives that now apparently mean something good happened.

The alcohol industry wants you to believe that simply drinking their specific brand of attractively packaged poison will turn you into the next Brad Pitt or Elle MacPherson. In reality, we know how good a drunk actually looks to us when we are sober. Whether they are male or female, there is perhaps nothing less attractive than having someone come up to you stinking of alcohol, slurring a badly thought out chat-up line, as a little bit of saliva drips from the corner of their mouth. Does it really make you a sex symbol if you have to use a drug to get the opposite sex to sleep with you? Forget the advertising spiel, the only way you can get you more sex while on alcohol is to find someone who is equally as drunk as you.

The more you think about what you are doing, the more ridiculous it appears. We create lots of distractions to avoid the truth about this drug. We claim it is essential to a good party; we think it makes food taste better, and we connect it to social standing. You must surely have heard that being able to pay astronomical amounts of money for your alcohol makes you a connoisseur and a person who appreciates the finer things in life (not an alcoholic). Listen to a 'wine expert' talk about the latest vintage to come out of the Bordeaux region, and you would think they were describing bottled sex. They talk of a seductive nose and a robust body with a hint of dark chocolate and wild berries.

As you will discover in this book, it's all just illusions created by the ego to keep you drinking by making you think it feels nice (or that it at least stops the unpleasant sensation of self-induced pain when you don't drink). Intelligent and wealthy people have simply found a way to put a veil of acceptability and snobbery over a common drug addiction.

Back when I was a drinker, I too got trapped into this illusion that finery and alcohol go hand in hand. I allowed myself to believe that the ritual of carefully selecting a very expensive bottle of wine from my temperature-controlled wine cellar, decanting the precious liquid into an exquisite crystal jug, then holding the glass aloft to admire the deep color and rich aroma meant that I wasn't a problem drinker; I was an expert admiring a piece of 'art'. Some of this art would cost me in the region of $500 a bottle.

Yes, we might have had to forego the annual family vacation to save money, but not surprisingly, my cellar was never forced to endure such austerity measures. My wine cellar was apparently never short of cash, even in the toughest times. Such was the depth of my delusion! I thought I had purchased those expensive bottles of art to impress friends, and yet they were normally opened while I sat alone after a bad day at work, trying to convince myself I deserved the liquid gold I was consuming. Daddy was 'not to be disturbed,' my wife would tell the children as they were stopped in their tracks en route to tell me about their exciting day at school.

I would take a noisy slurp of the fine vintage, drawing the air over the liquid on my palette, and write detailed tasting notes in my journal. Oh yes, I believed I was a connoisseur of the highest order and could hold my own with even the most seasoned of wine critics. But I was really just another druggy lying to myself in my basement.

One Friday evening, I took my wife at the time, Denise, out to an expensive French restaurant as a treat. As we walked into the elegantly lit restaurant, the sommelier recognized me, and his face lit up with a beaming smile. Walking over to us, he warmly greeted me and shook my hand, asking how I was and how the family was doing. He no more than nodded a welcome in my wife's direction before ushering us to the best table in the house. Before we had a chance to sit, he told me that he had just that week taken delivery of the 2003 Chateaux Pontet Canet. It was simply divine he assured me as he walked off to get a bottle.

Denise glanced at the wine list. This particular vintage was $350 a bottle. She gave me one of 'those looks' that perfectly conveyed her feelings about the matter. Words were not necessary. I knew what she was thinking. The kids need new school uniforms, and here I was considering blowing it all on one bottle of wine.

When the sommelier returned and proudly presented the label of the bottle to me, I explained it was a little too expensive. He nodded a non-judgmental smile but shot my wife a disapproving glance. He knew I was an easy sell, but there was an irritating voice of reason present who had spoilt it. He recommended a cheaper, but still expensive, alternative and poured us each a glass while we enjoyed our appetizers.

When our glasses reached a slurp or two away from empty, he returned with several more wide-bodied glasses, each with an inch or so of dark-colored, full-bodied red wine pre-poured into them. He placed them all down in front of me and, to my surprise and my wife's disgust, he pulled up a chair to join us. With his back to her, he sat beside me and pushed the first glass towards me.

'I would value your opinion, Mr. Beck. These are on the house. Just tell me what you think.' he said with a huge smile. If he could see the expression on the face of my wife, I doubt he would have been so cheerful!

It should have been clear to me that this guy had hijacked what should have been a romantic candlelit meal. In truth, I had never planned for it to be a romantic evening. It was just another evening activity that wouldn't interfere with my drinking. I could just have easily taken my wife to the theatre, but then I would have only been able to drink before the show and during the interval. A restaurant with alcohol on tap was a much better option, and besides, it was too late now. My ego had already kicked in; I was flattered to be considered such an expert that this experienced sommelier would value my opinion so highly. I felt about as significant as you can get. My ego was at pleasure level ten.

I picked up the vast glass, cupped it in the palm of my hand, and began the performance we wine aficionados like to give when consuming our favorite drug. I slurped loudly, rolled my tongue around, inspected the color against the candlelight and declared my verdict. 'Bravo!' He cheered, almost giddy with excitement at my approval. He pushed forward another glass, then another and another until a full thirty minutes had passed. I don't know how much spectacularly expensive wine I consumed gratis that night, but my, what a splendid evening I thought it to be.

I got home elated (and drunk), crowing about the extraordinary service and attention we had received all evening. My wife frowned at me and walked up the stairs to bed. She didn't say anything about the evening until the next time I suggested we go to the same restaurant. Her memory of the previous visit seemed to be in direct contrast with my own. She talked about the rude and unprofessional waiter who had ignored her all night and hogged my attention, boring her to death by droning on and on about his wine cellar. The scene she was describing shocked me; it was so far removed from what I had experienced. I even considered that maybe she had been there on a different occasion with someone else. I was much more willing to consider my wife was having an affair than that she didn't enjoy all the free alcohol we got that night!

Of course, her memories of the night were not clouded by vast quantities of a mind-altering drug. She was right, and I was just another problem drinker who had found a smokescreen to cover my habit. I was drinking one or two bottles of expensive, attractively packaged poison a night, but had managed to delude myself that there was nothing wrong in that. I couldn't have a problem because I was clearly a cut above the alcoholic in the park who chugged back super-strength tins of beer. I was buying and drinking the stuff of kings. This was an indication of my social standing and refined palette, and surely not a proclamation of a drug addiction!

Bullshit! Whether your smokescreen is the same as mine or you have managed to create another entirely different one, it's still just bullshit and nothing more. The sooner you grow up and admit this, the better. It doesn't matter whether you drink cheap plonk or expensive wine, it's all the same thing. Alcohol kills just as many intelligent and wealthy people as it does poor and deprived; it doesn't care how much you spent on your habit. The doctor won't cut you open one day and declare you to have the correct type of liver failure, and thank goodness you drank the posh stuff and not that horrible cheap cider.

Let me quote you what the World Health Organization says about your drug of choice, and then let me ask you if at any point they refer to the type or quality of the alcohol being consumed:

> The harmful use of alcohol is a global problem that compromises both individual and social development. It results in 3.0 million deaths each year. Alcohol is the world's third-largest risk factor for premature mortality, disability, and loss of health; it is the leading risk factor in the Western Pacific and the Americas and the second largest in Europe. Alcohol is associated with many serious social and developmental issues, including violence, child neglect and abuse, and absenteeism in the workplace. It also causes harm far beyond the physical and psychological health of the drinker. It harms the well-being and health of people around the drinker. An intoxicated person can harm others or put them at risk of traffic accidents or violent behavior or negatively affect co-workers, relatives, friends or strangers. Thus, the impact of the harmful use of alcohol reaches deep into society (World Health Organization, 2018).

Stop deluding yourself that you are part of something greater or a member of a special, elite club. A bottle of wine a night makes you no better than the homeless person swigging supermarket's own label whiskey in the park. Your bottle may have a pretty label, but inside, the poison remains the same.

You might assume that cigarette smoking is the world's biggest killer, and you would be correct. However, that fact is only true when you apply it to the full spectrum of social demographics. Low paid manual workers and the elite with their expensive Cubans and such add a disproportionate number to that figure. Actually, when you consider the middle-income earners, alcohol becomes the true grim reaper.

One of my favorite arguments to prove that I was doing nothing wrong was to state loudly and proudly, 'Hey, at least I don't smoke.' I would say this because I felt it proved that I could be doing something much worse. Of course, along with all the other lies I believed, this rationalization was just smoke and mirrors.

Alcohol is known as the silent killer because so many assume that they would be able to recognize the signs of a problem early enough simply to stop. The fact that they even consider this illogical nonsense as a safety net is evidence in itself that the mousetrap has already been primed. It's exactly the same as the mouse assuming he would have enough time to avoid the steel trap bar and its deadly spike before it got the chance to hit him.

With the problem drinker, this one assumption is the mother of all mistakes, because the organ most at risk of fatal damage from alcohol is the liver. This unique part of the body is a piece of natural engineering that way surpasses the label 'genius.' This one organ is responsible for hundreds of vital functions in the healthy human body. It even has the ability to repair itself and can continue to function with up to 70% of its surface area damaged.

The problem is, the liver has very few nerve endings, so the drinker is often unaware of the damage being done to the liver until it is severe. Only when the organ itself becomes so swollen from the abuse that it begins to press on other more sensitive areas of the abdomen do addicts begin to feel something wrong and start to worry they have caused some damage.

As I am sure you can appreciate, when a human organ is so badly swollen that it is pressing on other parts of the body with enough pressure to cause pain, it must be in a pretty shocking state. Sadly, it is often only at this point that people think about going to the doctor but often will put it off as long as possible for fear that (God forbid) the doctor insists that they stop drinking. Often by the time they reach the point where they can't sleep for the pain and can't avoid the doctor any longer do they go and get the tests. Many, at this point, find out that the damage is irreversible, and the only option is a liver transplant. So you get a liver transplant, and everything is fine again, right?

Wrong! There are currently 18,000 people in the United States awaiting a liver transplant. Where do you think you would rank on the waiting list next to the child who was perhaps born with a defective liver, or the woman seriously injured in an automobile wreck? Health services around the world don't look too kindly on people like you who had a perfectly good liver and opted to destroy it. Plus they assume that you will only go on to abuse the donor organ, too, and so you may never see the top of that waiting list.

So subtle is the drug that most problem drinkers are not aware of the precise moment that control was lost and they became alcohol dependent. There certainly is no point trying to work out when you changed from being a 'social' drinker of poison to an addicted drinker of poison.

The only fair assumption to make is that anyone who starts drinking alcohol socially inadvertently primes the mousetrap the moment they take their first sip. Some people will be destroyed by the mechanism and others may never feel the harm, but the only true way to ensure you don't get squashed is never to try and grab that cheese and stay well away from the trap in the first place.

Everyone who drinks alcohol is in the cycle. All those strangers, friends, and colleagues you wrongly assume are somehow better than you because they apparently can take or leave a drink are still all mice sitting blissfully unaware of the danger. The steel bar may snap closed on them next week, next year, in ten years' time, or maybe they will sit there for a lifetime. The only constant is, as long as they continue to consume the addictive drug alcohol, they continue to play a very dangerous game of alcohol buckaroo, and you have seen what happens when that mule eventually kicks!

Society insists that there is a profound difference between the people who drink a few bottles of wine a week and those who drink to excess on a daily basis. The latter are described as suffering from an illness called alcoholism; they are labeled as alcoholics and forced by well-meaning support groups to identify themselves by the same derogatory nametag. They are told that they have a condition that is incurable and must for the rest of their life describe themselves as a 'recovering alcoholic.'

Perhaps this bleak and depressing ritual explains why 95% of people who turn to organizations such as Alcoholics Anonymous fail to stop drinking. This book is certainly not here to put down the efforts of this organization, or any other method, because for the 5% of people who do escape from the loop using the Big Book theory of alcohol cessation, the rewards are truly life-changing.

The reason AA doesn't work for most people is that it requires its members to use willpower to quit. This is the default weapon for human beings when they identify something in their life that is not serving them. From trying to lose weight to giving up an addictive drug, we always assume the best course of action is to force ourselves to stay away from the thing we crave. The very idea of willpower is an oxymoron. There is actually no power at all in willpower.

Drinking alcohol is akin to juggling with fire sticks; there is a decent chance you will get burned. The difference in this comparison is that you wouldn't then label the people who got injured by the flame as incurable 'fireaholics.' We would be more likely to say that they, unfortunately, got hurt as the result of playing with a substance that, used in the wrong context, is dangerous. Using fire for anything other than cooking and heating is not a safe activity (exactly why we scold our children for playing with matches). Using alcohol for anything other than its chemically defined uses as a disinfectant, germicide, or fuel is asking for trouble. When trouble inevitably arrives with this use of this drug, we choose to blame the person and not the substance that actually caused the damage.

You are not an alcoholic, nor are you weak-willed or suffering from an addictive personality. You are none of those things. Over 80% of the western world consumes alcohol, and 80% of those people are no longer in control.

If you watch the glamour adverts for the latest designer vodka in high rotation across our television screens, you may find that hard to believe. Alcohol appears to be, if not the reason for the party in the first place, the life and soul of its success. Alcohol is potentially the most dangerous and deceptive drug on planet earth! Overdramatic? As we progress on this journey together, I will explain why this is the case.

Let me tell you here and now, you are most certainly not alone. Thousands and thousands of people just like you lose control of alcohol every day. That one little drink to help them unwind at the end of a busy day or the quick pint with friends has turned from a 'like-to-have' to a 'must-have.'

As with all drink-related problems, this doesn't happen overnight. You don't wake up one morning an 'alcoholic.' These problems develop slowly over 5 to 20 years, so slowly you don't even see them coming. Such is the viciously deceptive nature of this drug that initially there are no negative symptoms to indicate the beginning of a serious problem. As a matter of fact, for most people, the beginning of a long battle with alcohol will appear to be woven with an array of positives. Early-stage problem drinkers may feel lively, confident, and carefree when they drink. Eventually, they become known for being able to 'handle their alcohol,' as though this is a positive trait to be proud of. Often these people are described as party animals or the life and soul of any occasion. So while the chemical is working on your brain, your friends and colleagues are working on your ego, a powerful combination indeed.

Many people don't actually buy this book to stop drinking. They are hoping to prove to themselves and their caring friends and family who have expressed concern over their use of alcohol, that they don't have a problem. I can sugarcoat this next section for you if you wish. I could spend several chapters building up to it, but let's cut to the chase, and you can decide whether you want to disagree before we go any further together. Let me fire some questions at you:

• Have you ever planned your day based on the availability of alcohol?

• Have you ever made rules for yourself about your drinking, e.g., I will only drink beer and no hard spirits?

• Has anyone ever questioned you about your drinking?

• Have you ever tried to stop or cut down your drinking and failed before?

A 'yes' to any of those questions, my friend, means you have a problem with alcohol. I deliberately don't call you an alcoholic because I know your automatic conditioned response is to defend yourself in the face of such an assault on your perception of who you are. Regardless of how blatant the problem and symptoms appear to be, if you label someone an alcoholic, you will quickly get sold the line 'I admit I drink too much, but I am most certainly not an alcoholic.' I understand this objection because, despite the fact that I consumed on average over 120 units of alcohol a week for a period of nearly ten years, I still refused to declare myself to be an alcoholic. To this day, I point-blank refuse to accept that label. I do not believe any of the thousands of people who have stopped drinking via this method are either. You are no more alcoholic than an individual who is constantly scratching his head could be said to be a 'scratchaholic.' Alcohol misuse is the symptom of a problem and not the actual problem itself.

Many people think of alcoholics as disheveled, homeless winos who have lost everything, but there are people who meet the criteria for a medical diagnosis for alcohol dependence who are highly functional in society and still have their jobs, homes, and families. This type of drinker is known as a functional alcoholic (or functional problem drinker, whatever label you want to apply). They rarely miss work or other obligations because of their drinking, although it does happen occasionally. They usually excel in their jobs and careers. Typically, they are knowledgeable and witty individuals who are successful in many areas of their lives. To all but those who are closest to them, they give the outward appearance of being perfectly unremarkable.

I know who these people are because I used to be one. I kept my drinking hidden through some of the most successful periods of my career in broadcasting. If you also have a problem with this drug that is currently kept hidden away from your colleagues and family, I will show you throughout the course of this book how to take control of the situation without anyone needing to know you ever had a problem in the first place.

Free Coaching Video

If you are wondering if you really have a problem with alcohol or you don't know if you should quit completely or just cut back - watch this video:

https://www.stopdrinkingexpert.com/mailer-alcoholic/

References

World Health Organization (2018). Alcohol. *World Health Organization.* www.who.int/news-room/fact-sheets/detail/alcohol.

CHAPTER 2: DENIAL IS A PROBLEM AND NOT JUST A RIVER IN EGYPT!

Leugnen

At Bootcamp, I introduce myself as a former problem drinker. I explain that for two decades of my life, I had a severe problem with alcohol. At no point do I refer to myself as an alcoholic. The word is loaded with so many false assumptions. Indeed, I believe that label is one of the many reasons that Alcoholics Anonymous failed so badly for me.

Annahmen

You see, calling someone an alcoholic implies that there is something wrong or broken about them. Alcohol is the only drug where when you get into trouble with it, they blame you and not the substance. That doesn't happen with any other addictive drug. If you tell somebody that you are a smoker of cigarettes, they don't instantly recoil and insist that you will be forever a 'smokeaholic.' Even if you summon the

bedeuten

willpower to quit the filthy habit, you will only ever be a recovering 'smokeaholic.'

Getting addicted to nicotine is seen as the usual result of the repeated consumption of the drug. People don't assume you must be a terrible weakwilled individual. Even with illegal drugs such as 'heroin' people don't automatically believe the problem lies within the user. Society understands that drugs like heroin are viciously addictive and easy to get hooked on. Only with alcohol does the blame get placed on the drinker. Tell someone you can't control your drinking and watch their face drop. It's almost like you just told them you have terminal leprosy.

I am a logical thinker, and so things have to make sense to me for them to sit well. When I went to AA for the first time, and they told me that I would have to accept the fact that I was an alcoholic, and always would be I didn't like it one bit. I was a successful man in all other areas of my life. Here I was being told that I was a pathetic, broken individual who had no hope of recovery. This opening gambit of this well-meaning organization might be why I found alcoholics anonymous meetings to be so depressing.

Here's the logic of alcohol addiction, from my humble point of view. Alcohol is not a harmless social pleasantry, as the marketing might like to suggest. It is a dangerous, highly addictive drug that kills millions of people every year. Alcohol is the second most addictive substance on earth, just behind heroin. If you repeatedly consume it, over many years and wind up getting addicted, that should not suggest that there is something wrong with you. Getting hooked should be seen as the entirely logical conclusion of your actions.

There is nothing wrong with you! You are not weakwilled, broken, or pathetic. You drank a highly addictive substance, and guess what happened? That's right; you got addicted! As predictable as getting wet usually follows the action of jumping into a swimming pool.

At Quit Drinking Bootcamp, I get to see a huge weight lift off the shoulders of the attendees. The mood of the room changes; some people smile, others relax a little more into their chair. Why? Because what I just explained makes perfect, logical sense. However, it only takes a few seconds for a few of those smiles to turn into a confused frown. I know why that happens, and I know the question I am almost certain to be asked. Sure enough, a brave hand will raise to ask the question 'but, if that's true, why doesn't everyone get addicted, why am I sitting here and not my friends'?

It's a great question, and the answer is not clear-cut. [*eindeutig*] But the reality of alcohol addiction is it needs a lot of effort and persistence to get hooked. Firstly it tastes disgusting, that's why we have to start our drinking career with drinks loaded with sugar. For many people, they don't drink enough to get passed the problem that it doesn't taste very nice. Other people are slightly allergic to alcohol because their liver is not very good at processing it. In these cases, drinking alcohol makes them feel ill. Yes, I know it makes everyone feel sick, but for a lot, the negative side-effects are much more significant than you or I experience.

It's prevalent [*häufig*] for Asian people to be born with a severe allergy to alcohol, and consequently, they cannot drink at all. This sort of reaction is referred to as Asian Blush because drinking makes their face glow red. I had a Chinese friend in school called Andy Lee. He had this exact 'problem.' It sounds more of a blessing now, but at the time, he found it incredibly frustrating that he couldn't join in with the alcohol adventure we were all pursuing.

There was a small group of us who would hang around together. Our entire focus was split between girls and alcohol. Unfortunately, I was much more successful with alcohol than I was with the girls. As I was the tallest and looked the oldest, I was the member of our group most likely to get served in the local pubs and liquor stores. We would pool our money, and I would nervously buy the cider and alcopops. Then we would head off to a nearby derelict building to sit around drinking and laughing.

Andy would attempt to keep pace with us, but within a short time, his face would turn bright red, and he would start to feel dizzy. We all ruthlessly mocked him by suggesting we didn't even need a campfire to keep warm or toast marshmallows. We could use the fiery glow coming off Andy's face. He hated that he couldn't drink like us and at the time we were all very grateful that we didn't have Andy's problem. Isn't hindsight a beautiful thing?

Imagine if you got the hangover, not the next morning but twenty minutes after starting drinking. How many people would need a book like this, never mind taking a weekend out of their busy life to attend something as crazy as a Quit Drinking Bootcamp? In summary, alcohol is highly addictive in people who give it a chance to take hold.

I talk about my 20-year problem with alcohol, but I have to admit that for the first decade, I didn't believe I had a problem. I was proud of my reputation for being a man who could 'handle his drink' and saw myself as a very sociable and popular individual. I was always the first to the bar, and I got invited to a lot of parties. Why? Because I was very good value. I would turn up with extra alcohol, in case you didn't have enough. I would drink quickly and get slowly drunk. I would get cheeky, then funny, then rude before having to be scraped off the floor and put in a taxi and sent home to sleep it off. I was the outrageous, funny drunk that people would laugh about the next day around the water cooler.

However, if during this period of my life, you had accused me of having a problem with alcohol, I would have got very angry with you. I would have made statements that today I see clearly as nothing more than warning signs of pending alcoholism. You would have heard me shout you down with 'hey, I can stop anytime I like' and 'keep your nose out of my business, it's my body, and I will do what I want.' Of course, we know all too well that drinking is never just a problem for us alone. Alcohol hurts everyone you love; it damages every aspect of your life and the lives of those in your little bubble.

It wasn't until my health started to go downhill that I realized I had a problem. However, I still didn't want to quit drinking; I always believed I was in control and could moderate my drinking somehow. I wasn't out of the denial I was finding ways to dig myself a bigger hole. Even with alcohol causing massive damage to my life, I wasn't looking for the exit. I was looking for plausible deniability to justify my actions. I didn't want to quit drinking; it was the best thing in my life. It seems insane to even write that sentence now, but at the time, I believed it. All I wanted was to enjoy one glass of wine a night and put the bottle away for another day. I had seen friends do this magic trick, and it amazed me. I couldn't understand how anyone could have an open container of alcohol in the house and not drink it.

This was my utopia; this was the dream. Even when my liver started to fail, and I was under the care of consultants at the hospital, this was still what I wanted. I tried everything to achieve it. The peak of my denial saw me come up with the stupidest invention ever thought of... the drinker's safe!

One morning I had what I believed to be 'a genius' idea. I ordered a huge time delay safe. Costing over $1000 this was the sort of secure box that banks have installed. A few days later it was delivered on the back of a flatbed truck and installed into my home. I programmed the safe to only open for 5 minutes at precisely 6 pm every day. The theory was, I would keep all my alcohol in the safe. I would arrive home from work and pour myself a single glass, and before taking a drink, I would close the safe, sealing it for another 24 hours. I would have my drink but be unable to get access to anymore.

It worked! I was so impressed with myself. I thought I was a genius. I even started to think about how I could market this amazing product. I saw myself pitching to the investors on Dragons Den or Shark Tank. For about two weeks, my idea worked perfectly. I would have my drink and sometimes go and try to open the safe to get another but was never successful. Fantastic!

The whole concept fell apart one Friday evening when as I was leaving the office at 5.30pm, my boss saw me and called me into his office for a chat. He had a project for me to work on the next week and wanted to give me the heads up. I sat there in his office nervously staring at my watch. I said yes to everything he suggested, regardless of how much extra work it would involve. I just wanted him to shut up and let me get the hell out of there. Finally, at 5.50pm, he let me go, and I sprinted to my car, furiously driving home, taking every shortcut I could think of. Unfortunately, I wasn't quick enough, and I arrived home at 6.05pm just as my safe sealed itself for another 24 hours. I screamed at the ceiling; I shouted at my wife, and the dog wisely disappeared out into the back yard.

I was furious, I felted cheated, and that life wasn't fair. I grabbed my car keys and drove to the liquor store and bought a bottle of whiskey. At that moment, my genius idea that was going to change the world became a $1000 embarrassing waste of money.

What an idiot!

So, when you come to Bootcamp feeling nervous and ashamed, don't! No matter what you have done to cover up your denial, I have been there done it and bought the t-shirt.

One of the main reasons that problem drinkers seek help for their drinking problems is the eventual negative consequence of their alcohol consumption. When the pain or embarrassment gets bad enough, they can no longer deny that their drinking needs to be addressed. For the functional problem drinker, the denial runs deep, because they have yet to encounter outward negative consequences of their habit.

They go to work every day. They haven't suffered financially. Most have never been arrested or on the wrong side of the law. From their point of view, they simply can't have a problem because they don't fit their definition of what a person with a drinking problem should look like! Don't blame television, Hollywood, or its actors. They are compelled to keep portraying alcoholics as the staggering, slurring down-and-outs that we are familiar with. If a director instructed his leading man to play an alcoholic character as a functional alcoholic, how would we even know he had any sort of addiction problem?

The functional problem drinker often consumes just as much alcohol as any fully blown alcoholic, they just don't exhibit the outward symptoms of dependence. This is because they have developed such a tolerance for alcohol that they must consume much more to feel the effects. Consequently, they must drink increasingly larger amounts to get the high they crave. This slow build-up of alcohol tolerance means the functional alcoholic is drinking at dangerous levels, which can result in alcohol-related organ damage, cognitive impairment, and alcohol dependence. Chronic, heavy drinkers can display a functional tolerance to the point that they show few obvious signs of intoxication, even at high blood alcohol concentrations, which in others would be incapacitating.

In the mid-1990s, Steve McFadden, a popular British soap opera actor, was arrested and charged with driving under the influence of alcohol. He had consumed nine double vodkas before getting behind the wheel of his car. While to most people, this would be enough to knock them out for the night, he decided to fight the prosecution because he claimed to have had an unusually high tolerance to alcohol. The courts witnessed the bizarre scene of a man consuming such a vast amount of drink and still appearing to be completely sober. The judge obviously bought the argument as the actor was banned for just 18 months, a very light sentence for such a large blood alcohol reading.

You need to change what alcoholic means to you. It doesn't mean you must accept being a social outcast or that the condition is permanent. Alcoholism isn't a figment of your imagination, and I will keep confirming for you that you are not weak-willed or in any way a failure because of this problem. To which you are probably responding, 'Why can't just open a bottle of wine and have one glass with my meal?' or 'Why can't I ever just have one, like my friends appear to be able to do?'

If alcoholics were weak-willed individuals, wouldn't that flaw in their personality apply to all areas of their life? If there is really such a thing as an addictive personality, then logic would dictate that the condition would apply to all areas and all alcoholics would also be obese, gambling-addicted, heroin-injecting, glue sniffers. You are alcoholic because of a long-term chemical imbalance exacerbated by your body's tendency to process alcohol differently from those annoying people who can just enjoy a glass of red wine with their steak and think nothing of putting the bottle away for another day.

Alcoholism is referred to as a disease, just like cancer. This is not true; calling it a disease implies there is nothing you can do about it and that you may have contracted it through absolutely no fault of your own. This creates the innocent victim mentality that drinkers then use as a perfectly valid excuse for them to continue drinking to excess. Once labeled as such, they begin a 'pity party' that can last a lifetime. They declare how terrible it is to suffer from such a debilitating condition, shrugging their shoulders, cursing their bad luck as they wash away their perceived problems with a stiff drink.

You have lost a fight that you never had any chance of winning. It is not your fault, but it absolutely is your responsibility.

Problem drinking is not a disease; it is a negative behavioral loop that appears to be so complicated that it may feel as though it is unbreakable. Many people state that they drink to make their problems go away, but at the same time, they are aware of all the extra problems their drinking is creating. All your beliefs about why you drink are likely to be a Catch 22 situation.

For example, you are worried about money and don't want to spend the evening thinking about all those bills, and so out comes the alcohol. The alcohol (which is a mild anesthetic) merely time shifts your problems forward another 24 hours and then adds the problem of alcohol withdrawal into the mix. Remember, you started drinking to forget the bills, but the alcohol habit is costing you thousands of dollars each year, and if you didn't spend so much feeding your alcohol addiction, you would probably be able to pay all the bills you are worrying about in the first place.

The average person who stops drinking as a result of reading this book or through my online course and coaching goes on to save over $4,000 per year. While money isn't, strictly speaking, a good enough reason to stop on its own, it is a very pleasant by-product of quitting. If you were offered a no-strings pay rise of that size, wouldn't you gladly accept it?

If saving money is only a byproduct of the process, you might be wondering what the primary reason is. We will come to that in due course. But I urge you not to try to skip ahead. At this point, it's important to read this book in the order it is written and not be tempted to skip ahead to look for the magic bullet cure. You will find no such thing; it is the slow deconstruction of the lies alcohol has repeatedly told you over the years, and a growing understanding of why alcohol affects you the way it does that allows you to see it for what it is. More importantly, you will need to stop believing that alcohol is somehow benefiting you.

There are no real benefits of drinking alcohol, only illusions of positives. Everyone who consumes alcohol has inadvertently placed themself in the mousetrap. Some are moments away from disaster; others are a lifetime away. Slowly the mechanism is loaded and primed. Over time, you become more at risk of letting alcohol seize control of your life. You are effectively playing a virtual version of Russian roulette, with alcohol as the bullet in your loaded gun. Every time you drink you pull the trigger, and one day the chamber will not be empty. There is only one way to play this game safely, and that is to remove the bullet — or to put it another way — don't drink.

This killer product escapes virtually all of our current regulations and safeguards because it has been around long enough to set its own precedent. The fact that 'everyone drinks' and our parents, grandparents, and generations as far back as we can recall also drank alcohol makes us incorrectly believe we are protected by the assumed 'safety in numbers' principle. Actually, that is not true. No drinker really believes that he or she is protected because of the social proof of the drug; they are just pleased to have another weapon in their arsenal to justify their behavior around a substance that we all inherently know is dangerous and unhealthy.

There is no safety in numbers with alcohol. Just because everyone you know drinks does not make alcohol a safe product, nor reduce your chances of getting addicted or suffering harm in some way. Whether one person plays Russian roulette or a billion people play, the odds remain the same for each person holding the gun. Every pull of the trigger is a separate unique incident and is completely independent of and uninfluenced by all the other triggers being pulled at that time. Just because the people who surround you all appear to be 'in control' of their drinking does not give you license to assume that you are in control.

Many people pick up this book, still hanging on to the hope that they will be able to reduce their drinking down to a sensible amount. I would love to tell you that glorious compromise is possible. Perhaps I would sell more books if I pretended that it is. However, integrity is important to me, and I can't tell you anything but the hard facts and truth about this drug.

Reducing the amount of poison you are consuming is as helpful to you as closing an open porthole on the Titanic. If I were to advise you to cut down, there would be an implication that drinking perhaps provides some benefits if consumed in small amounts. It doesn't.

The most common objection to this statement comes from the 'red wine is good for your heart' brigade. Credit where it is due, this is correct to a certain degree; there are indeed a lot of healthy antioxidants in a glass of red wine. But no more than you would find in a glass of non-alcoholic grape juice, or a hand-ful of pomegranate seeds. If wine is so good for your heart, why don't doctors break out the merlot when a patient is rushed to hospital suffering from a heart attack? If it's your heart you are concerned about, find an alternative to wine. But if you really are using that argument to continue drinking, I suspect it really has nothing to do with your health.

When most people realize drinking has changed from a 'nice-to-have' into a 'must-have,' they try to cut down. If you had a reckless and thrill-seeking friend who you discovered was in the habit of loading a single bullet into a revolver and playing Russian roulette for kicks a few times a week, would you really advise him to cut down and only do it on the weekend or to stop completely?

Throughout the course of this book, I am going to demonstrate

unbestreitbar

to you in undeniable detail exactly why alcohol does not serve you, has absolutely no benefits, and creates nothing but negative consequences in your life. As the intelligent human being that I know you are, I am sure you will come to understand that everything you currently believe is just smoke and mirrors
Blendwerk
generated by a myriad of social and psychological sources. Once you understand this, you won't need my help to stop drinking— you simply won't want to.

We start this journey together by discovering exactly why people drink alcohol to excess. Some will claim alcohol has uplifting qualities. This is simply not true as it is actually a mind anesthetic). Others will say they need it to chill out and relax, and you will discover later why this is equally illogical. At this moment, all you need to know is that there is only one reason why people get hooked on alcohol: It's an addictive drug that causes a chemical imbalance in the brain.

There are no other reasons. You are not a victim of a disease or prone to an addictive personality. There is no such thing as an addictive personality. It's just a convenient way of shifting the blame away from us to something external and apparently outside of our control.

If somebody who juggles knives was accidentally stabbed by one of them, would you say it was not his fault because he has a personality that is susceptible to knife injuries? Or would you assume it was bound to happen one day?

If you take an addictive substance, you will get addicted; it is an automatic and logical conclusion to your actions. It was bound to happen one day. It has nothing to do with a perceived fault in your genetic makeup. Surely if such a broad condition as an addictive personality really existed, then you would be addicted to everything. You would consume mountains of mashed potato, vats of honey, kilos of sugar, and so on, apportioning all blame to your damn addictive personality disorder.

The closest excuse you have to your drinking not being your fault is a possible genetic blip in your DNA that makes you pre-disposed to be highly likely to develop a problem with alcohol. Breakthroughs in a field of medical science called epigenetic inheritance have revealed some startling findings.

Meeri Kim, writing for the Washington Post, says:

> A newborn mouse pup, seemingly innocent to the workings of the world, may actually harbor generations' worth of information passed down by its ancestors.

> In the experiment, researchers taught male mice to fear the smell of cherry blossoms by associating the scent with mild foot shocks. Two weeks later, they bred with females. The resulting pups were raised to adulthood, having never been exposed to the smell.

> When the critters caught a whiff of it for the first time, they suddenly became anxious and fearful. They were even born with more cherry-blossom-detecting neurons in their noses and more brain space devoted to cherry-blossom-smelling.

> The memory transmission extended out another generation when these male mice bred, and similar results were found.

> Neuroscientists at Emory University found that genetic markers, thought to be wiped clean before birth, were used to transmit a single traumatic experience across generations, leaving behind traces in the behavior and anatomy of future pups.

> The study, published online Sunday in the journal Nature Neuroscience, adds to a growing pile of evidence suggesting that characteristics outside of the strict genetic code may also be acquired from our parents through epigenetic

inheritance. Epigenetics studies how molecules act as DNA markers that influence how the genome is read. We pick up these epigenetic markers during our lives and in various locations on our body as we develop and interact with our environment.

Through a process dubbed 'reprogramming,' these epigenetic markers were thought to be erased in the earliest stages of development in mammals. But recent research, this study included, has shown that some of these markers may survive to the next generation.

In the past decade, the once-controversial field of epigenetics has blossomed. But proving epigenetic inheritance can be a daunting, needle-in-a-haystack undertaking. Researchers need to measure changes in offspring behavior and neuroanatomy, as well as tease out epigenetic markers within the father's sperm.

The DNA itself doesn't change, but how the sequence is read can vary wildly depending on which parts are accessible. Even though all the cells in our bodies share the same DNA, these markers can silence all the irrelevant genes so that a skin cell can be a skin cell, and not a brain cell or a liver cell.

Does this mean we, as humans, have also inherited generations of fears and experiences? Quite possibly, say scientists. Studies on humans suggest that children and grandchildren may have felt the epigenetic impact of such traumatic events such as famine, the Holocaust, and the 9/11 terrorist attacks.

We are still scratching the surface of this new and exciting research, but what this helps to explain is why children of alcoholics are much more likely to also to develop a problem. Whether it is genetic inheritance or social conditioning is a point that will be debated for years. What this doesn't mean is that you can carry on drinking while pointing an accusing finger at your parents. If you discovered that skin cancer runs in your family, would you sit in the midday sun every day and then blame your mom and dad when the bad news arrived one day?

The main reason your drinking has become a problem comes down to a deficiency of important chemicals in your brain. Inside your frontal lobes, there are millions of transmitters and receivers. These control every aspect of your life and determine how you feel about literally everything you experience on a day-to-day basis. When the sun goes down at the end of the day, the decrease in available light causes your brain to stop producing adrenaline and start manufacturing a neurochemical called melatonin. This clever chemical calms your mind and allows sleep to occur. If you take a substance that interferes with this natural process, such as caffeine, then you will find it very difficult to get to sleep because of the chemical imbalance.

Staying with the sleep example for a moment, there are a few other reasons why the chemicals may not be present in the quantity that you need for a healthy regular sleep pattern. The brain makes melatonin from another chemical called serotonin. This is what makes us feel good about ourselves; it's a happy drug naturally created by our body to manifest feelings of contentment and joy. Serotonin can only be made from an amino acid called tryptophan. If your diet is poor or specifically lacking in foods that are sources of tryptophan, then you will have a serotonin deficiency. As a direct result of that, you will also have a melatonin deficiency. In the short term, you would experience having trouble sleeping. If this imbalance continues, you begin to label yourself an insomniac.

The other way you can have a chemical imbalance (again staying with the sleep analogy) is by being genetically predisposed to it. If you are born with tryptophan transmitters and receivers that do not work as well as they should, then you will need to consume significantly more of the amino acid in your diet than a 'normal' person to get the same result.

Imbalanced brain chemistry makes you miserable!

Alcohol is a toxin that interferes with brain chemistry. Imbalanced brain chemistry makes you unhappy, unsettled, stressed, and tired — all negative emotions that you believe can be fixed with a glass of the good stuff. This is a negative behavior loop like picking at a scab because it hurts. The more you pick at it, the worse it gets, and yet you just can't leave it alone. You are stressed because alcohol has created a chemical imbalance in your brain, so you have a drink to unwind. The alcohol goes on to create more chemical imbalances to ensure that you also feel uncomfortable again the next day, ensuring the consumption of the drug continues.

If you owned a multimillion-dollar racehorse, is it fair to say that you would treat it with respect, stable it in the very best yard and feed it only the best premium food you could buy? Is it also equally reasonable to assume if you owned this valuable racehorse, you probably wouldn't put poison in its food? You own a body that is quite frankly awe-inspiring in its beauty, complexity, and power, and yet you deliberately consume poison and claim you do it in the name of being social.

Thankfully, as a result of millions of years of evolution, your body is pretty smart. It can sense when there is a dangerous foreign substance in the bloodstream. When you ingest any toxin, your body will start a series of automatic processes to eliminate it from your system (as many a late-night cab driver has discovered). First, the liver converts the alcohol into another chemical called acetaldehyde, which is less dangerous to the vital organs. Alcohol-dependent people have slowly trained and conditioned their liver to become far too efficient at processing alcohol. No sooner has the alcohol flowed into their liver than it is processed into acetaldehyde. This means we problem drinkers always have vast quantities of this chemical in our blood.

This causes two major problems. First, it acts as an opiate, which, as you know, is highly addictive (we effectively have to deal with a continuous drug overdose). Second, at such a high level, these powerful chemicals rip through brain cells like napalm. It interferes with thousands of receptors, prevents your body from absorbing minerals and vitamins, and interferes with brain chemicals to such an extent that it takes months for the body to repair the damage (if you would just give it a chance).

When alcohol hits your brain, it triggers an artificial release of powerful chemicals that create a high. Every time you use alcohol to simulate this response, the receiver in your brain responsible for detecting the chemicals gets damaged a little bit more. This is why, over time, you need more alcohol to achieve the same effect you used to get from one drink. This tolerance to alcohol is often seen as something to be proud of, especially in men. Being able to knock back ten pints of strong lager and not fall over has apparently become a clear sign of a real man. Remove the testosterone, and in reality, tolerance is the first clear sign that alcohol has already caused significant damage.

Because of this severe chemical imbalance, you are predisposed to having a problem with alcohol, so using willpower to try to stop is always going to be like pushing oil up a hill. Fighting brain chemicals with willpower is pointless; if you have ever had a general anesthetic, you will know that when they inject you with the chemical, they assess its effectiveness by challenging you to count to ten. You confidently begin the count, but somewhere around four or five, the lights go out. Even if you wanted to fight the drug, you would lose. There is no power in willpower!

This rule applies as much to naturally generated chemicals as it does to artificial ones. If your brain is full of adrenaline, you can't go to sleep. It is impossible, no matter how much will-power you use. Specific chemicals in your brain create all strong emotions from grief to love. Estrogen makes women want to mother and care for the young; testosterone makes men want to fight and have sex with things; dopamine creates a feeling of contentment, and so on. If you injected someone with adren-aline just before going into a cinema, it would be unreasonable of you to call him weak-willed because he wouldn't sit still and watch the movie with you.

Willpower is completely ineffective against brain chemistry. In order to stop drinking you are going to have to change the way you think about alcohol. You are going to have to get to a place where you genuinely don't want to drink again. And for that to happen, you're going to need to become aware that al-cohol slowly turns us all into liars. We are programmed from a very young age to perceive alcohol as a faultless, natural, mood-enhancing, confidence-inducing, 'good times for all' product and not the foul-tasting, health-destroying, slow poison that it really is. You're going to have to become aware of the lies.

Before we go any further, I need to remind you that I am not a doctor. Neither am I a self-righteous saint who has never put a foot wrong on the path of life. I am not here to judge you or heap a load of shame upon you. I am here with you now because, in essence, I am the same as you. I, too, let alcohol control my life for over 17 years. The only difference between you and me is that now I am sitting outside the mousetrap looking at you sitting on it, like a greedy mouse that thinks he has discovered something amazing. Because I have been in the trap and experi-enced it, I know how you feel about giving up the drink. I know how many hundreds of times you have woken up ashamed of yourself, making veiled promises never to drink again. I know that you desperately want to give up this poison, but I am also deeply aware that at the same time, the thought of spending the rest of your life without a drink appears at first thought to be a life not worth living. The fact that you are reading this book means at some level you still believe that alcohol is a benefit to you. If you didn't believe that, then you simply wouldn't drink and you wouldn't need me.

For most alcohol-dependent people, a life without a drink appears empty and pointless. You may even be tempted to throw out objections such as:

- I can't go to a party and not drink!
- I would be a boring, party-pooper for the rest of my life.
- There's no way I could go through a holiday without drinking.
- But, I have to drink to relax and steady my nerves.
- You can insert your own lie here if you want — but that's really all it is — a lie!

While you can't physically see any of the particles that make up the air that we breathe, you know that it is a mix of different gases, with oxygen being the most vital. You can't point to oxygen and prove its existence to me, but if I approached you today and told you that there is no oxygen in air, you wouldn't give any credence to my claim. Unless you are a physicist, this probably isn't because of your irrefutable scientific knowledge or your ability to prove the existence of oxygen at the drop of a hat. It is purely because people you respect and trust have taught you this. You have been programmed to believe this from a very early age. The belief that we breathe oxygen is so ingrained into the collective wisdom of society that it has become an undeniable fact.

Similarly, for thousands of years, it was a statement of fact that the earth was flat. Repetition is the mother of learning, and so beliefs that have been repeated and observed many times over and by many different people become hard-wired facts in our collective intellect.

Alcohol and celebration are natural bedfellows, right? All of our perceptions of alcohol come from society's collective opinion of it. Just as we were wrong about the earth being flat, we are collectively incorrect about what alcohol gives us. Some drinkers are so well programmed that at the mere suggestion from me that alcohol is not the nectar of the gods but rather a foul-tasting, life-destroying drug, they will instantly and aggressively disagree. If you find yourself saying 'Well, that's wrong. For a start, I genuinely do like the taste of alcohol, ' I can promise you here and now, you are at the point where your lies are so profound and so deeply ingrained in your subconscious that you can't even tell they are lies anymore.

With that depressing assessment established, I want to give you two big reasons to be excited about where you are. First, you not only bought this book but you opened it and started reading. This might sound like no big deal, but let me tell you that over half the people who pick up a book to help address their drinking problem never even open it! Second, I am going to show you how to beat this drug in a completely easy and pain-free way. Stay with me for the rest of this book and I will prove to you not only that alcohol is vile tasting but that all the rest of the things you believed about alcohol are lies, as well.

Once you begin to see alcohol for what it really is, you won't have to do anything. Stopping drinking will become the by-product of your new knowledge – it will happen automatically.

Free Coaching Video

Watch this video to understand the warning
signs that your body may be giving you.

https://www.stopdrinkingexpert.com/pain-in-your-side/

WHY DO YOU DRINK?

It might seem like a strange question, but nobody is drinking out purely out of habit. Alcohol appears to be providing a benefit. At the start of the book, I asked you to grab a pen and write down your reasons to drink alcohol. Don't worry; I know that 99.9% of readers didn't do it; if you did, I am super impressed. Either way, let me ask you again.

At Quit Drinking Bootcamp I ask the same question, here are the seven most common answers:

Alcohol Helps Me Get To Sleep

I understand this reason totally; I used it myself for many years. In fact, I would get very grumpy if I had to attend an evening event that prevented me from drinking. I would kick and scream like a fussy baby, complaining that, as a result, I would be awake all night. However, it's so easy to prove to ourselves that alcohol does not help us sleep well. We choose not to see the truth.

If it were true that alcohol helped with sleep, then all problem drinkers would wake up every morning full of energy and vitality. You would see them at work skipping to their desk, so refreshed and well-rested. However, we know that is not the case. Indeed it's the opposite of the truth. The problem drinker has to drag themselves to their desk and urgently call out for coffee before they can even find the energy to raise their head.

Alcohol helps you get to sleep because it's a mild anesthetic. However, is it not true that after a few hours you wake up again. Your heart is pounding in your chest, and you feel dehydrated and clutch your aching head as you stagger to the toilet. Perhaps you have a drink of water and stumble back to bed, where you spend the rest of the night tossing and turning and generally having poor quality sleep. This continues until the alarm clock screams, and you can't believe that you have to go to work feeling so utterly exhausted.

Alcohol promises you that it will help you with insomnia. The truth is alcohol causes sleep disruption.

Drinking makes me more fun to be with:

Again this feels like it could be accurate, but it is easily disproved by merely being the sober person at a drunken party. Alcohol doesn't make people more fun; it makes them more stupid. If aliens visited planet earth and observed a typical party from start to end, the observation would send them retreating to their homeworld with nothing but pity for the human race. They would have seen reasonably intelligent individuals gather at one location and immediately choose to drink the discharge from rotting vegetable matter. This will seem like an act of stupidity but will turn out to be the tip of the iceberg.

The aliens will watch as these humans repeat the exercise over and over again until they can no longer speak properly. They will observe someone telling the same story five times in a row. The people listening, instead of highlighting the repetition will react to the story as though it is the first time they ever heard it. As the party progresses, some of the 'friends' will start fighting with each other. Some will fall over and hurt themselves, and there is always the one person who does something wholly inappropriate and embarrassed themselves. A few will be so drunk they will need to be helped into a taxi and sent home to vomit into the toilet.

The next morning all members of the party will wake up feeling like death and update their social media status. They will declare the evening to have been great fun and a huge success. They will report that Jenny was hammered, Tim was slaughtered, and Nick was a total mess - but all that means very good things happened. The aliens conclude we are a planet full of morons and hastily leave.

Alcohol does not make you fun; it makes you stupid. Let me assure you; you came here with gifts, talents, and a mission. You won't be laying on your death bed, feeling grateful that you opted to live a bit chunk of your life with the intellectual capacity of a chimpanzee.

Red wine is good for your heart!

I love the passion that drinkers have for this lie. It is the very embodiment of confirmation bias. People see a story on Facebook that states 'Merlot found to be good for cardiovascular health' and they like and share it like they just discovered the holy grail. Not for a moment, do they even consider it might not be true?

A few months ago a lady emailed me to triumphantly declare 'I was just about to join your online quit drinking program and I discovered that red wine has now been proven to be beneficial for your heart! What have you got to say about that Mr. Stop Drinking Expert'?

It's not true.

That's what I have to say to that. And the fact that a statement is not true is always the most significant defense to any argument. The whole red wine is good for your heart story started as an off the cuff comment by a news anchor on an American evening news program. The channel was running a story about some very poorly constructed research. It had been conducted to try and find out why French people had such a significantly lower level of cardiovascular disease than the population of the United States. As it turns out, the reasons were not clear cut or obvious, so the researchers made an assumption. That fact alone should serve to highlight how inadequate this study was. The conclusion was lept to that French people drink more red wine than Americans, and therefore that must be the reason they have better heart health.

Entirely spurious and very unscientific, but the conclusion sat well with the news anchor, who came off the back of the story and raised a pretend glass to the camera. As the credits started to roll, he made an unscripted comment along the lines of 'that's a good enough reason for me, cheers.'

With that silly, throw away comment the alcohol industry went crazy. It had just been on the nightly news that red wine is good for your heart. 'Big Alcohol' got their marketing and PR teams working overtime to get the message out that if you care about your health, you would do well to start drinking more red wine.

Absolute and total garbage based on incomplete data, but it's a story that's been kept alive for the last thirty years. Thanks to social media, it's not going to disappear anytime soon.

This whole premise was finally put to bed last year by Cambridge University in the United Kingdom. They concluded using research for an exhaustive 600,000 people; there is not only zero health benefit to drinking red wine, but there is no safe amount that can be consumed. Even one drink a day will result in a shorter lifespan. However, you are unlikely to see this robust correction shared on Facebook so much. Why? Simply because it does not provide any plausible deniability to the millions of problem drinkers around the world.

If red wine was really good for your cardiovascular health when you have a heart attack and get rushed to the emergency room. The doctors would urgently put you on Merlot, stat! Wouldn't they?

But they don't, because it's not true.

Dutch courage gives you confidence: Zuversicht

Does drinking make you more confident? There is a swift answer to this question...No! Alcohol really gives you stupidity, and there is a big difference between the two.

People *believe* that they feel more self-assured and confident when they have had a drink. There is even common parlance for it "Dutch Courage".

'It's one of those expressions we use without giving much thought to where it came from. In numerous ways, the Dutch used to be Britain's dearest neighbors. From the rise of the United Provinces throughout the sovereignty of Queen Elizabeth I and up until the eclipse of the Netherlands as a major power in the Napoleonic conflicts. They were sometimes enemies but more usually co-religionist allies, significant trading associates and irregular provincial rivals. Even more than that a Dutchman, William, even went on to become king of England in

1689.

These connections between the two countries have forced the word "Dutch" to appear repeatedly in the English language. Slang dictionaries have plenty of phrases such as 'going Dutch', 'Dutch auction', 'Dutch uncle' and of course "Dutch Courage".

'Dutch courage' has a pair of possible origins. The first derives from the denigrating idea that *Johnny Foreigner is a weaker chap than the firm and sturdy Englishman*. Whether this bounder was cruising up the Medway or facing down the locals in the East Indies, he required a handful of drinks before a battle.

The second idea relates more directly to the use of a specific alcoholic beverage "gin" to bolster one's "confidence or bravery" in battle.

Gin in its contemporary form, was reputedly invented by the Dutch physician Franz de le Boë in the 17th century. British troops fighting Louis XIV together with their allies in the Low Countries appreciated the calming influences of Dutch gin before heading into battle.

Whether it expressly referred to gin, 'Dutch courage' as an English colloquialism tended to mean using spirits, not just beer, to reinforce self-belief.

This all sounds very poetic and romantic, but the real story is less so. Front line soldiers in these sorts of battles were really nothing more than cannon fodder. They were considered the affordable and expendable casualties of war. They were the poor sods that would charge into the first and most gruesome line of defense while the opulent generals sat at a safe distance on handsome stallions looking on.

However, willingly charging toward your gruesome dismemberment and eventual death 'doesn't so much need bravery or confidence. 'What's needed is a good dose of stupidity and poor decision-making. It just so happens that alcohol is perfect for inducing both these mental states in a person. **Alcohol was the ultimate tool to manipulate men to die for their country.**

'Here's the hard reality. One of the reasons why alcohol is so good at what it does (successfully killing someone every minute or every day). Is because they very first thing the drug does is disable the section of the brain responsible for making sound decisions. This is why people find it so hard to have just one drink and then stop. While sober, you have the seemingly unbreakable determination just to have one little drink. However, as soon as the drug plays its first hand, you become as weak and vulnerable as a newborn baby.

This effect on the logic areas of the brain is also the reason why people become less risk-averse after drinking.

Becoming less able to gauge risk does not make you confident it makes you stupid. So yes, you may have had the "nerve" to approach the hot girl after you had had a drink but 'don't kid yourself that you were acting bravely or even more confidently.

No beautiful woman ever looks at a drunk man, who is clumsily trying to pick her up and thinks "wow he is so confident". The inebriated chump who firmly believes he can jump from one hotel balcony to the next, is not being super confident.

There is no such thing as Dutch Courage. Alcohol makes you stupid. I would argue that in most of the occasions where alcohol is used for so-called Dutch Courage. For example, making a presentation at work, going for a job interview, talking to a man or woman you are attracted to, etc. Perhaps deliberately making yourself progressively less intelligent is about the worst possible choice you could make.

'Don't you agree?

It's dangerous to stop drinking:

When I write a blog article about stopping drinking, there is always at least one person who objects, stating that quitting drinking without medical supervision is lethal.

This is a significant subject and before we get into it, let me give you a disclaimer. I am not a doctor, and I do not offer medical advice. I am a former problem drinker who has helped many thousands of people to escape the trap of daily drinking.

Before you make any significant changes to your lifestyle, you should, of course, consult a GP.

All that said, there is an essential distinction between the stereotypical alcoholic you see portrayed on TV and in the movies. And the type of functional alcoholic that ends up at the Stop Drinking Expert website.

Most people who are addicted to alcohol are not so hooked that they can no longer function in society. They are not the disheveled hoboes you see sitting on a park bench swigging cheap brandy from a bottle hidden inside a brown paper bag.

End-stage alcoholics are entirely debilitated by their drug addiction. They can't go more than a few hours without a drink. For this reason, they can no longer hold down a job, provide for their family, or drive a car. Their whole life has been taken over by their addiction.

These people virtually never end up on my website mainly because they are not functional enough to decide that on their own.

Alcoholics of this nature are not suitable for my approach to alcohol addiction. They are way past the sort of help that I can offer – they need urgent inpatient medical care.

It is true that if someone this addicted to alcohol stopped cold turkey, they would suffer terrible withdrawal, and may even die without medical intervention.

However, this is not a reason for people to keep drinking. The myth that cold turkey = instant death is a fear that is propagated by the alcohol manufacturers and other problem drinkers. The alcohol producers operate deviously and dishonestly just the same way the cigarette manufacturers do.

Alcoholic beverage companies fund research, propaganda, and marketing that spread 'fake news' (I hate that I just used that phrase). Such stories as 'red wine is good for your heart,' 'moderate drinkers live longer than nondrinkers' and of course 'cold turkey is dangerous.' All these are 100% proof bullshit in most cases.

Most people who discover the Stop Drinking Expert website are entirely functioning drinkers. They are good parents, partners, and successful career people. Many have never missed a day of work because of their drinking, and their driving license is clear of DUI's.

My members are not weak-willed, broken, or uneducated. Actually, I have found precisely the opposite tends to be true. The vast majority of my members are incredibly intelligent and successful individuals.

My members are not getting up each morning and reaching for the whiskey bottle. However, they probably are drinking between one and two bottles of wine every night. Despite the propaganda being drip-fed into a society that suggests this level of drinking is risk-free. I can tell you from experience if you sustain this level of drinking for several years, you start to experience devastating consequences.

This level of drinking dramatically affects your finances, health, relationships, and career. Most people drinking to this level feel completely out of control. They wake up every morning, wracked with guilt and regret. Despite how miserable alcohol is making them, they simply can't stop drinking it!

For these people stopping drinking will not cause them to drop down dead suddenly. Their withdrawal experience is mostly insignificant. Often no more than a mild sensation of anxiety and perhaps a few sleepless nights.

The chemical withdrawal from alcohol takes a couple of weeks. This unpleasant but entirely bearable sensation reaches a climax around 24-36 hours after quitting and then slowly fades over the following 14 days.

If your drinking pattern fits the functioning alcoholic description, I have just given then withdrawal is not a reason to continue drinking, sorry!

If you experience any physical symptoms such as trembling and vomiting etc. then, of course, your first course of action should be to visit your GP. Even in these rare cases, it isn't a license to carry on drinking. The doctor will give you some medication to make the physical withdrawal symptoms more tolerable, so you can continue the process.

The alcohol manufacturers are hiding their secret and devious mission under the gloss of expensive and carefully designed marketing. Don't fall for it!

Warning that cold turkey is dangerous may appear at first glance to be a caring advisory, but there is more to it than that. Telling someone who is addicted to a drug that if they stop, they will die makes them feel stressed and anxious.

Guess what people addicted to alcohol turn to when they feel stressed... yes that's right – they drink!

I genuinely like the taste of it:

Most people who drink wine every day claim they honestly like the taste of it. This is nonsense; alcohol tastes so bad that the drinks manufacturers mostly have to find increasingly potent ways to cover it up. The body is an amazing and sophisticated piece of natural engineering.

Despite what lies you have taught yourself on a superficial level, you still cannot break the rules your body has created over millions of years of evolution. Right at the top of our hierarchy of needs is the need to protect life, to stay alive at all costs. This is hardwired into every cell, every molecule and every tiny atom of your being. You can't decide to stop your heart beating or never to breathe again. You can't because it breaks the ultimate built-in rule; that of ensuring self-preservation at all costs.

The reason pure alcohol tastes terrible is the same reason rotting meat or moldy, fungus infested bread tastes terrible. Your body is warning you that you are consuming something that is putting you at risk. Think about it, in a hospital operating theatre, the room and the entire medical team that works in it must be 100% free of germs, bacteria, and viral contaminants. So what do they scrub their hands with; not soap but alcohol. Because instantly, on contact with any living organisms, it kills them dead! It pulls every bit of moisture out of their cells and causes them to implode in on themselves. At a microcellular level, alcohol is akin to thermonuclear war; nothing survives.

Do you honestly believe you have some fantastic internal system to get around this fact? Somehow, when you consume this dangerous disinfectant, it 'doesn't do the same level of damage because you have hidden it in a bit of cranberry juice.

Alcohol tastes horrible, you already know this but have forgotten, or as is more accurate, you have conditioned yourself to believe the opposite. As a hypnotherapist, I can tell you that this is entirely possible and can be easily replicated in a relatively short space of time to prove the point. In hypnosis, the conscious (thinking and judging) mind is bypassed, which means I can speak directly to the subconscious and implant beliefs without interference from the ego. Obviously, in therapy (and what you will find on the hypnosis tracks that accompany this book – available in the member's area) all suggestions are positive and delivered for your benefit, but it is entirely possible for me to condition you to enjoy something deeply unpleasant, such as a hard punch on the arm! If while under hypnosis, I hit you hard but told you it felt amazing and repeated that process many times and over several sessions, you would eventually begin to crave the experience.

You can see this feature of the human mind demonstrated in the most horrendous situations. When people are held captive by a sole individual and despite the fact that this person has abducted them, tortured and abused them, the victim slowly over time begins to develop feelings for the perpetrator.

Despite suffering at the hands of this person, they become conditioned to their environment and begin to want to please the person who holds them against their will. This phenomenon has been studied at length by eminent psychologists and is known as "Stockholm syndrome".

To a certain degree, I believe you are suffering from a form of this syndrome; alcohol has abused you for so long that you now firmly believe there is a benefit to you. You have fallen in love with a killer!

I say again, alcohol tastes bad; your first interaction with it proved that point. When you first sneaked a drink of your 'father's neat whiskey, did it taste amazing? Or did it taste vile? Most people will say it tasted disgusting and they 'couldn't ever imagine getting hooked on something that tasted that bad. The taste of alcohol has not changed, so the only explanation for your current belief that it tastes good, is that you have changed. You have conditioned yourself to believe alcohol tastes good. 'Don't feel bad; you have had a significant helping hand from society and the advertising industry.

What you must understand from this point on is that what you previously believed about alcohol was a lie and nothing more. If I poured a glass of pure alcohol and asked you to dip your little finger in and taste it, I am sure you will agree it would taste horrible, indeed, if you drank that glass of liquid you would shortly be dead.

Funny really because since birth you have been programmed to ignore this and instead believe that alcohol is natural and an everyday part of life that you must consume if you are to be considered by your peers as a fun and social member of the gang. This is a throwback to our primitive evolution, we are still pack animals to a certain extent, and this is another reason for our global addiction to this drug.

The second reason is best explained by a smarter man than I, a famous psychologist called Abraham Maslow. Maslow is known for establishing the theory of a hierarchy of needs, writing that human beings are motivated by unsatisfied needs and that certain lower needs need to be satisfied before higher needs can be.

Although there is a continuous cycle of human wars, murder, and deceit, he believed that violence is not what human nature is meant to be like. Violence and other evils occur when human needs are thwarted. In other words, people who are deprived of lower needs, such as safety, may defend themselves by violent means. He did not believe that humans are violent because they enjoy violence. Or that they lie, cheat, and steal because they enjoy doing it.

According to Maslow, there are general types of needs (physiological, safety, love, and esteem), and they must be satisfied before a person can act unselfishly. He called these needs "deficiency needs". As long as we are motivated to satisfy these cravings, we are moving towards growth, toward self-actualization.

Satisfying needs is healthy, and blocking gratification makes us sick and unhappy. In other words, we are all "needs junkies" with cravings that must be satisfied and should be satisfied. If we don't concentrate on doing this, we will literally become sick.

"Will-power" is an illusionary weapon created by the egoic mind. 'It's like your enemy giving you a plastic sword and saying "here, use this to protect yourself if I ever attack you!" This is exactly why people have such a hard time trying to go cold turkey with their drinking. One morning you wake up and say, 'that's it I am never drinking again. By lunchtime, you have a psychological itch so intense you are almost screaming inside.

Will-power does not work because it forces your subconscious and conscious mind into civil war. The exact same reason why the moment you go on a diet, you become hungrier than you thought possible.

Here is the secret to stopping drinking; you need to attach more pleasure to not drinking than there is to drinking. You have to remove the need by understanding the truth about alcohol. It is not a social pleasantry but rather an attractively packaged poison. A multi-billion dollar marketing campaign for the alcoholic drinks industry is working exceptionally hard to convince you otherwise, but you have to trust your gut on this one.

Let me put the point another way. I have two wonderful children who I love and adore more than life itself. Maybe you also have children yourself, and you can understand my love and need to protect my children from the harms of the world? Let me ask you a question: If you had some strong rat poison for dealing with a tricky vermin infestation, would you keep it in a chocolate box and put it within reach of your kids?

Of course not! But alcohol is packaged exactly like that. It's just poison is sold in pretty elegant bottles. Surely something in such exquisite packaging must taste amazing right?

I need alcohol to relax:

One of the most common statements I hear from people I love is 'I only drink to relax.' They will defend this routine with extreme passion and the total confidence that they are in the right. In reality, the sense of relaxation comes from the removal of the withdrawal symptoms and nothing else and so if these people didn't drink in the first place there would be no artificial 'relaxation' required at all. However, this is the first illusion of alcohol.

The drinker feels stressed after a hard day at work, takes a drink, and suddenly feels better. It is understandable as to why they would connect the two events together and believe that the alcohol fixed their problem – what an amazing liquid! It's harder for the drinker to see that the alcohol used sleight of hand to set up the pain they are now feeling a day or so earlier. The kick from the drug alcohol lasts fourteen days and reaches a climax around twenty-four hours after the last consumption. So this means if you drink a glass of wine, for two weeks the drug is going to apply pressure on you to drink again.

The next day you will feel stressed and uncomfortable, most find a reason to explain this such as a hard day at work, unexpected bills waiting for them when they get home or disagreements with friends and family. Virtually no drinker correctly identifies this sensation as the kick being generated by a drug they consumed the previous day. So the trusty Pinot Grigio is opened and as quick as you can click your fingers the stresses and strain of the day all magically appear to vanish. What the drinker has really done is make a little deal with the devil. They have time-shifted the kick forward another twenty-four hours. The devil makes good on his side of the deal, and for now, they are at peace and feeling grateful to the magic liquid that caused the release from the pain.

The first glass leads to another, and slowly, the anesthetic nature of the drug takes hold. A few years ago I had an operation on my hip. As I lay on the operating table waiting to be wheeled into the theater, the anesthetist reassured me that I would be asleep during the whole process. Sound quite pleasant doesn't it? Sadly it's not true, general anaesthetic does not induce sleep but rather a reversible coma. Cerebral activity is slowed down to something close to brain stem death, rendering the patient unconscious and completely unaware.

There are no dreams to remember upon waking from a general anesthetic, as the brain was not capable of creating anything so complicated. Sometimes the doctor will inject the drug and challenge you to count to ten to help them monitor how it is taking hold of your senses. Even the most determined individual rarely gets past a count of five before the lights go out.

We see the same defiance in the face of alcohol. You almost certainly have seen drunk people insisting that they are 'as sober as a judge', offended at the very suggestion that they are smashed out of their minds. Police officers who pull over suspected DUI offenders watch over and over again as intoxicated fools try to fruitlessly demonstrate how in control they are. The moment you drink alcohol, you surrender control to the drug, you cannot change the way your body responds to this anymore than you can control gravity.

Alcohol makes the electrical activity in the brain become inconsistent and haphazard as neurons misfire, and receptors fail to respond correctly to commands. Simple everyday processes of the human body, such as walking and talking, become difficult.

The drinker finds their vision is blurred and shifting unnaturally as the brain struggles to process the data coming from the ocular system correctly. As a result walking becomes too challenging. Defeated by something they mastered at the age of ten months, they slump into their favorite chair, drink in hand. Speech becomes slurred and inconsistent; the drinker can often be surprised by the noises that are coming from their own mouth in place of the words they were trying to form.

Alcohol regresses the drinker to the capabilities of an infant, without any of the cuteness. They stumble around trying to walk; words are slurred and incomprehensible, often reducing the individual to basic grunts and noises. For all intents and purposes, you have a brain dead zombie for a companion.

This is not relaxation any more than you could claim to be really relaxed during a major operation!

Getting clear about the reasons you drink is important. Once you start taking each justification apart and finding out for yourself that there are no foundations to it. The power alcohol has over you starts to weaken. No longer does it feel like you are in a vice like grip but being held in place by the hand of some-thing no more powerful than that of a scared baby.

CHAPTER 3: WHERE IS THE POWER?

In the 1980s, when my friend's father had a new computer installed at his business premises, we all gathered in the street to watch its arrival. It was so large, the entire roof of the building had to be removed to accommodate its installation. It arrived on the back of a flatbed truck and was hoisted into position with a crane that had also been hired at great expense to complete the delivery. An entire office had been cleared and made available for it, and yet it was capable of no more than the basic functions of our modern-day calculators. In the realm of information technology, we have progressed a long way in a short time, to the point where we now casually carry mobile phones with ten thousand times the computing power than that goliath of a machine.

You only need to look back at some of the predictions made for computers by the popular science magazines of the day to realize just how much we have exceeded expectations. At one point, it was predicted that the worldwide market for computers would be just five machines, while another publication proudly declared that one day, all computer would weigh less than one-and-a-half tonnes!

Today the machines our children use just to play computer games on have infinitely more processing power and memory than the machines we used to thrust the first man into outer space.

However, despite these advances, we have still only created a device with less than 1% of the power of the human mind. You can learn even the most complex computer languages within five years, and yet you can spend a lifetime not comprehending the possibilities of your own internal computer.

Programmers spend years in training, diligently understanding the power of their machine before they start to generate code of any value. One of the first concepts they learn is through the acronym GIGO, which stands for Garbage In, Garbage Out. Sadly, most people don't apply the same discipline to programming their internal computer, a machine with the power to create literally anything.

Everything that you believe is wrong with your life exists purely because of bad programming in your subconscious mind. If you are overweight and unhappy about the size or shape of your body, it is due to a subconscious level belief that you want to be in that state. That's right I am saying if you are fat, then it's probably because your subconscious believes that's what you want! Many will object in the strongest terms to a statement like that, but you can't possibly know at a conscious level what is stored in your subconscious mind. It would be akin to claiming you can carry the world's oceans in an eggcup. For the moment, I would ask you to suspend your disbelief and stick with me as I explain.

A dependence on alcohol and other drugs is partly due to the unconscious belief that those chemicals are the best way to deal with pain being generated by your conscious thoughts. The perception that being seen in an expensive and flashy looking sports car makes you look more important to other people is a scenario generated by your egoic mind that has been repeated enough to become a subconscious belief. Perhaps from this point on, it may be better to refer to these types of beliefs as nothing more than a lie; the word 'believe' even has the word 'lie' in the middle of it as a reminder. The ego will attach itself to anything that hints at power, control, or permanency. It is the part of you that is afraid of death, and it will spend your entire life in a blind panic about that one event. If it can demonstrate in any way that you are more significant or more in control than other people, then it will do just that.

When desires of the ego become so embedded in our image of ourselves, they become automatic or subconscious. This is dangerous and self-destructive because of the immense power of the subconscious. The subconscious has a direct line to the divine power of the soul.

STOP! I feel an objection coming on, 'If the subconscious has the power of the soul, why doesn't it prevent the bad instructions from being completed? Why on earth would it sit back and allow a self-destructive program like alcoholism to run?' First, let me assure you I am not about to go 'all spiritual' on you just because I mentioned your soul. There is no religious element to this cure, but let's look at facts to understand how our brain operates fully.

It is commonly accepted that our mind is split into two unequal halves: our conscious (which we will call our thinking mind) and our much larger, more powerful subconscious. These two halves allow us to experience life on contrasting levels.

Nothing portrays the delusion of power held by the conscious or egoic mind, quite like the story of a little dog named Biba. Biba was the nasty little Jack Russell Terrier my girlfriend had when I was 16 years old. This dog had a serious attitude problem. It was no bigger than a sofa cushion was aggressive and believed that it was a fearsome Rottweiler. Every time I would visit my girlfriend, admittedly hoping for a bit of alone time with her, Biba would sit in the window watching me walk up the path to the house. Before I even had a chance to knock on the door, he would launch its pathetic and laughable attack. Occasionally I would see a flash of his little white needle-like teeth through the letterbox.

Once inside, he would sit on my girlfriend's lap snarling at me. This one-foot-high, ten pound, deluded animal actually looked at me, a 6'1', 14 stone man, and thought 'Just let me at him and I will rip him to pieces.' The reality, as Biba often discovered, is that he was so small I could remove him from the room without even bending over. Simply by placing my shoe under his belly I could lift him and carry him out into the kitchen on the end of my foot, his legs kicking and teeth snapping all the way. With a grin across my face, I would lock him in before sauntering back to my girlfriend, all the way listening to the furious muffled barking. For her sake, I would agree with her that he was indeed a little cutie; I didn't believe that letting her know my true feelings for this repulsive little rat would have done me any favors.

Biba is how I see the conscious mind; it is a small, inefficient part of your mind that thinks it's much bigger and more important than it really is. It also has all the decorum and attitude of that little dog. Your ego is the voice in your head that judges and questions everything in and around your life.

As a child, as you stood on the starting line of the school race and the ego was there whispering in your ear. What is whispered is unique to you and what your ego wanted at that moment (some believed they could win – and they did; some believed they couldn't – and they lost).

The voice begins quietly and grows as loud as you will let it. Ever-present in all areas of your life: at home, work, and even socially. When you walk into a bar as a singleton, it is the voice that tells you that you are more attractive and good looking than that person, but less so than another. As you watch a person drive past you in the automobile of your dreams, it is the voice that tells you how you should feel about that person's public display of success. It either views the scene as something that you should also have (and need to be happy) or as an example of your lack of self-worth. Of course, both assessments are pointless and do not serve you, but the ego is constantly looking for things to attach itself to. Books such as Rhonda Byrne's *The Secret* try to make you aware of this instinctive reaction of the ego, and instead of responding as the ego dictates, it encourages you to make positive statements of intent, suggesting instead of feeling envy, you see yourself sitting in that car and enjoy the positive image you have painted in your mind's eye.

This approach is laudable and certainly better than any negative emotion, but again, if it is purely willpower arguing with the ego, it is largely pointless. It is for this reason that so many try the techniques described in *The Secret* and other 'law of attraction' books but give up when they see little evidence of success. The real secret of manifestation is to understand that only the subconscious can create. And it does this in spite of the continuous diatribe coming from the ego. In short, you can say anything you want about yourself; it doesn't make the slightest bit of difference to what you get (unless you believe it). I can wake up every morning, stand in front of the bathroom mirror, and with all the confidence and positive mental attitude I can muster, state that I am a professional football player. Unless I subconsciously believe that is even possible, then the chance of it becoming a reality is somewhere between slim and none.

On one side of the coin, this appears frustrating that we can't manifest our desires so easily, but on the other side and with some knowledge of the perfectly horrendous scenarios our thinking mind can create, it's probably for the best. Have you ever stood on top of a tall building and wondered just for the briefest of moments what it would feel like if you fell? With that in mind, ask yourself, do you still want to give the conscious mind the power to manifest the stuff of your imagination?

We all allow the ego to become so vocal that we begin to believe that it is who we are; we actually become the voice in our head. This is ultimately the source of all unhappiness and discontentment in life. The ultimate illusionist responsible for all the pain, but a master at laying the blame elsewhere, all input from this voice is generated by the need to avoid fear. With that in mind, it's not difficult to see why egoic dreams and indeed any desire born of negative emotion, is unlikely to be beneficial in the long run. The conscious mind simply can't stop judging and answering questions, even if it doesn't know the answer. Such is the predictability of the ego that I can demonstrate its weakness with a few statements and questions that I would like you to try NOT to answer.

What is 2+2?

What color are your eyes?

Whatever you do, don't think of an elephant!

Like a puppy chasing a ball, your conscious mind cannot help itself; it simply must answer all questions asked of it. This isn't entirely a problem, as, without this feature of the human mind, you would be dead by now. While your conscious mind comes up with some pretty ill-advised opinions about you and what you need to be happy, it also does a job of protecting you by judging all the situations in which you find yourself on a daily basis.

As you stand on the side of a busy road waiting to cross, your conscious mind evaluates the speed and distance of approaching traffic and decides at what point it is safe for you to cross the road. The reason why young people and the elderly are more at risk of injury in these situations is further evidence of the weakness of the ego. Children do not have enough information to judge the risk accurately, and the elderly are using outdated perceptions.

The conscious uses what it believes to be true to make the judgment. No doubt, at some point when you were a child, you picked up a hot pan on the stove and discovered quite quickly how much a burn could hurt. The lack of knowledge meant your conscious mind was incapable of judging the situation as a threat, but from that point on, you will be much more cautious in the same environment. Taking this into consideration, you may now feel some gratitude towards your ego for acting so effectively at these points and saving you from serious harm. However, you should also be able to see that they are all motivated by nothing positive but rather the simple desire to avoid pain/fear. Everything the ego does comes from this starting point, and it is unwise to mistake its protection for care, the ego has no regard for your best interests, it only cares about what it wants. Sometimes the by-product of what the ego desires coincidently serves your 'well-being' at the same time, but it is not there by design; you just got lucky on that occasion.

The ego is quite willing to cause you immense suffering purely to get to the outcome it desires. Should the ego desire a specific material possession (or rather the feelings generated by attainment), it will apply massive pressure in the form of emotional pain until you give it what it wants. Then, of course, as soon as you comply, it rewards you briefly before beginning the process over again with even more intensity. This book is taking you on a journey of awareness, and part of that is developing the ability to observe the ego as a third person trying to manipulate you rather than believe that you and your ego are one and the same.

If by this point you are not feeling too schizophrenic, let's talk about the larger and significantly more powerful subconscious. A polar opposite to the ego, the unconscious mind judges nothing; it is completely at peace and feels no need to compare you to others. It wants nothing, needs nothing, and fears nothing, operating in a divine state, existing purely at the moment. Nothing that has gone before is relevant, and the future is considered equally unimportant. The only thing that has relevance is the now, and in each and every moment, your subconscious dutifully completes the programs that reside within itself with perfect accuracy. This is why you don't have to consciously beat your heart, control your body temperature, or any of the other millions of functions happening in your body every second of every day.

During the time it has taken for you to read that last sentence, your subconscious has destroyed and replaced 50,000,000 cells in your body; its power is simply awe-inspiring. Ridiculously, sitting at the feet of the awesome power and like Biba, the bad attitude dog, your conscious mind actually believes it is equal to, if not more powerful. This is the very embodiment of arrogance and pomposity. It's like a three-legged, blind donkey insisting it could take on and beat a multimillion-dollar racehorse. The truth is like a bully challenged to really show what he is made of. If your ego suddenly became responsible for everything currently looked after by the subconscious, you would be dead in less than a second.

Why do most people in the western world drink?

Because the conscious mind contains the ego, and the ego is insane! It creates all the misery and then comes up with completely ineffective ways to deal with the problems. It lives in a constant state of pure terror, always trying to manipulate you to make that fear dissipate. Like a whirling dervish in a fine china store, the ego stumbles through life predicting doom and gloom. It creates chaos and then points the finger of blame at someone else, anyone else. As you respond to this drama and try your best to avoid the tidal wave of destruction the ego would create, given a chance, you experience these sensations as evidence of life is difficult, hard and a constant struggle.

Spiritual souls such as monks and Buddhist teachers know that resisting the demands of the ego and being at peace with whatever happens in this lifetime are the secret to true happiness. They know at a deep and profound level that life is not the beginning or the end, but rather a continuation, and so the ego loses its leverage over them. When their ego screams and shouts about whatever material possession it has decided they should have to be truly happy, these enlightened folk ignore it and simply stay quietly in the moment. This does not mean their life is easy or that they don't suffer, but they do choose to accept responsibility for all of life's challenges rather than seek to blame and struggle to retake control.

Sadly the vast majority of us are not able to recognize the ego because we have become too interlinked with it. We believe the judgments and demands in our head to be our own, and we respond accordingly, thrashing about trying to control the uncontrollable. It inevitably makes us miserable and stressed. Alcohol sedates the conscious mind by acting as a brief distraction. All addictions serve the same purpose, whether it is overeating, drugs, or the modern and trendy conditions, such as Hollywood's new favorite, 'sex addiction.' It's a bit like when you pretend to throw a ball for a dog. For a few seconds, the dog runs off in the direction you pretended to throw. It stops and looks around for the ball before realizing it was a trick and then it comes pouncing back to you.

You are using a chemical distraction for the ego! So why alcohol for you and not something else, you might ask? That is a question with a million answers, but you can be sure it's no accident. Genetics and your environment undoubtedly play a part, but these all cause the same problem: a chemical imbalance in the brain. If you can prevent the imbalance and change your belief structure around alcohol, you will be cured.

I do not deny that DNA plays a part. You are indeed significantly more likely to have a drinking problem if your parents were dependent upon alcohol. This could be the result of picking up equally ineffective transmitters and receivers as your parents had, or purely due to a psychological trait called social proof, i.e., the tendency to accept as true what you repeatedly witness by those around you.

If you grew up watching your father come home from work and before he even got his hat and coat off, a large whiskey was gripped firmly in his hand, it's not difficult to see why you would develop the belief that this is normal behavior. If your father (whom you respect and admire) uses alcohol and appears to enjoy it so much, then it must be a benefit that you are currently being deprived of. Your ego will not accept that situation, and as soon as it can, it will correct that injustice. This is why at the age of 12, you find yourself sneaking a sip of your dad's whiskey and wondering why it tastes so awful.

It is also equally likely that you have inherited the same over-efficient liver and ineffective receptors in the brain that most alcoholics are a victim to. When most people take a drink of alcohol, it causes the hypothalamus in the brain to release a powerful neurotransmitter called dopamine. For most people, those 'goody-two-shoes types' who appear to be able to have a glass of champagne at a party without desperately looking for the next one, the dopamine release is tiny. It creates a small sense of well-being, but there is not enough chemical excreted and quickly enough to be addictive (in your sense of the word).

To give you a non-alcohol related comparison, imagine if some people were similarly desensitized to sweet and sugary food like chocolate or cake, as you are to alcohol. Imagine, for these people with a 'cake tolerance' to get the same taste and enjoyment that you get from a single piece of chocolate cake they would have to eat 30 slices (just to get the slightest hint of the kick you get). Do you think any of them would get addicted? It's very hard to get hooked on something that requires that level of interaction. This is why alcoholism carries such a stigma. For most people it seems like completely nonsensical behavior. In exactly the same way that you would frown at and chastise, someone who shoveled down 30 pieces of cake in a sitting.

In the problem drinker, more often than not, the dopamine released as a response to the detection of alcohol in the bloodstream is massive. Suddenly the body is awash with huge quantities of a powerful and addictive drug. So much so that the sheer onslaught of chemicals damages the receivers in the brain in the same way that continuous loud noise causes damage to hearing. People who have worked with noisy machinery all their lives have a diminished ability to receive sound at the correct level and need to be fitted with a hearing aid to amplify the volume. Drinkers have a diminished ability to receive neurotransmitters and need higher quantities of the drug to recreate the original high.

The chemical receptors in the brains of those who are dependent on alcohol are so numbed from the 'noise' of the continual abuse that they simply cannot detect the feel-good chemicals produced by the body at natural levels. Only when a drug creates a massive flood of the chemicals are they able to feel 'normal.' The good news is, if you stop drinking, within a few weeks you will start to feel better, and within six months to a year your receptors will be repaired.

The easy option here is to declare that your drinking is not your fault; you are cursed with a defective hypothalamus. Nice try, but this only explains why you choose to be dependent on alcohol rather than having a different addiction. In other words, if it wasn't the alcohol, it would be something else. The problem lies not with the alcohol, but with your ego or conscious mind believing it is in control of your life. The ego has selected alcohol to address an underlying problem, and this is why I say you are not an alcoholic. Your use of alcohol is a symptom of a problem, not the actual problem itself.

All worry, anxiety, stress, and depression come directly from the conscious mind's delusion that it can predict the future. That little voice inside your head that comes up with a thousand things that could go wrong is simply the ego trying to punch above its weight. The ego is also the hidden voice that judges you and deems you unworthy of some things based on experiences of the past. Girls who grew up with abusive and controlling fathers often go on to marry abusive and controlling husbands. This is a pure manifestation of the ego using the past to try and predict the future.

The ego, unable to accept its own lack of power, tries in vain to control the uncontrollable. Every moment of life is experienced in the present, right here; in this moment, neither the past nor the future exists. Those enlightened souls who live their lives in the moment NEVER, and I really do mean NEVER, have addictions.

Having no concern for the past and not knowing what the future might bring, is pure chaos to the egoic mind, and it simply can't accept it. You will no doubt have heard of the human drive to apply order to chaos, well this comes directly from the conscious mind trying to predict the next series of events using the past as a reverse projector (assuming what went wrong before will happen again).

Does this sound crazy or schizophrenic?

Good, because it is! The ego is insane, and its continuous dissatisfaction with life and its never-ending lists of needs, desires, and fears cause the running dialogue in your mind that makes you crave alcohol as a panacea. Drinking hits the pause button on this monologue, and for a brief moment, the pain stops, the dopamine sedates the ego, and you take a small step towards peace. The futility of using any addiction to pause the tape, so to speak, is that when the fix wears off, the tape begins to play again; you haven't missed any of the gloomy recordings. At no point did you fast forward. You still have all the pain to go through from the moment you hit pause. Plus, you now have the additional problem of withdrawal from an addictive drug and the chemical imbalance that comes from that.

By now, you should be able to see why willpower has been so ineffective in the past. One of the biggest problems with willpower is the associated feeling that you are a bad person or doing something wrong. Then ultimately, when you fail to force the bad habit into abeyance, you are left with the demoralizing sensation of failure and hopelessness. Let's get this straight, just because you are struggling with alcohol addiction does not mean you are a bad person or a failure. Think of it like this:

Sleeping tablets make you fall asleep, anti-emetic tablets stop you from being sick, and addictive drugs get you addicted. It would not be your fault if you fell asleep after taking a sleeping tablet, and therefore, we must apply the same blame to alcohol and not to you.

Alcoholism is a symptom of the problem and not the problem itself! The complexities of why we get addicted to anything are hugely misunderstood. The route out of this destructive cycle has nothing to do with drinking, what you will learn as we progress through this book, is that the cure for your problem lies here at this moment, and is not some future destination you will arrive at one day.

Free Coaching Video

Getting addicted to alcohol has nothing to do with your intelligence, gender, or social standing. Watch this video to discover how intelligent and successful people fall for the trap of alcoholism:

https://www.stopdrinkingexpert.com/intelligent-people/

CHAPTER 4: YOU ARE NOT ALONE

More than 80% of the adult population of the western world drink alcohol, more than 80% of those have a problem, and 80% of them will never admit it. The first thing you should be proud of is that you have taken a step that most people will never have the courage to take. You have admitted that you are worried. Not only that, you have paid your hard-earned money and put your trust in my system to help you regain control of your drinking. I can't express this strongly enough: this small act puts you in the top 20% of people. Admitting you have a problem effectively means you are already 50% of the way down the road to full recovery.

STOP! Before you break open the champagne (or whatever your chosen brand of attractively packaged poison is), let me give you a word of warning: Despite what you have been told in the past, knowledge is not power, but rather, knowledge is only potential power! If you do nothing with it, it's useless data. The shocking fact is that 20% of the people who buy a self-help book such as this one will never even open the it to the first page. It's as though the act of buying the book was good enough 'for now.'

It's similar to the act of procrastination by all of those who proclaim, 'The diet starts Monday!' Surely, if they were committed to losing the weight, they would start the diet immediately, without delay! The diet always starts Monday because it's a free license to eat like a pig all weekend while lying to yourself that you have all the right intentions in the world to repair the damage on Monday. By the way, the reason diets don't work for 95% of the people who try them is because they also require willpower which so often fails, leaving them unhappy and fat.

Now that you have started on this monumental journey, do not stop. Neither should you skip forward to try and find the secret or quick fix to your problem. You did not go to bed one night in control of alcohol and wake up the next morning a problem drinker. This drug has taken years, sometimes even decades, to alter physical pathways in your brain. There is no quick fix, but that doesn't mean it has to be painful, or that you need to suffer. The adage of 'No Pain—No Gain' does not apply here, and trying to fight your way out of this situation is actually why you have failed to cut down in the past. It's going to take some effort on your behalf, and you may mess up every now and again, but it's not a big deal. You are not a robot, and as long as you stick with this process, you are going to end up stronger, cleaner, and happier than you have been in a long, long time.

Unless, of course, you are STILL asking the question 'Do I have a problem with drinking?' That is the question I get asked more than any other. If I had a penny for every email I have received from people describing their habits and then asking, 'Do you think I have a problem?' I would be well on my way to a very happy retirement.

Let me answer that question for you now by first translating the question into what I believe you are REALLY asking: 'I like drinking, but I am worried I can't stop. Can you tell me I don't have a problem and make the worry go away so I can carry on?'

You have an unnatural relationship with alcohol, and that is why you are here. Regular 'social' poison drinkers don't ever think about their drinking habits, never mind search the Internet for help and advice, or go as far as to purchase a book like this. If you have to question your behavior around alcohol, it's the clearest sign you can get that alcohol has become a fixation. Try not to beat yourself up about this because, in reality, it's not possible for anyone to have a natural relationship with alcohol because it is a toxin packaged in pretty bottles. The belief that anyone can be a 'normal/social' drinker of poison is a myth. How can it be possible to be a typical user of an addictive drug?

If a friend confided in you that he was a glue sniffer, but has kept his solvent abuse strictly limited to weekends, would you declare him a 'social' glue sniffer? Replace glue with heroin. Would your friend be a 'normal' heroin user? You may think I am going to extremes to prove a point here, but there are only two differences between alcohol and heroin.

The first difference is social acceptability. Drinking is socially acceptable, and heroin is not. From birth we are exposed to alcohol being portrayed in a positive light, a substance that we are happy to ignore the logic of, and assume that it has some sort of smart technology behind it.

Somehow we believe alcohol can make us more aware of positive emotions and feelings, and claim it can also dampen down negative emotions and help us forget our problems. Only a substance that could change its chemical make-up could achieve this. There is nothing intelligent about alcohol. Remember, it is the waste product of decaying vegetable matter, not a lab-designed smart drug.

The second difference between alcohol and other class A street drugs is the amount of time it takes to become addicted. It is effortless to become addicted to heroin in a short space of time because the kick (withdrawal) begins so much more quickly after the drug is discontinued than with alcohol. Heroin users experience massive and unbearable amounts of pain in a relatively short space of time.

That is where the differences end. They both can, and will, try to kill you. They will both do significant permanent damage to your health, relationships, finances, and state of mind, and they will both twist your perception dramatically enough to make you believe that regardless of all this harm, they are also in some way a benefit to you.

I believe that alcohol is infinitely more deceptive than heroin because of the long and drawn-out way it drags the user into a trap. Alcohol dependency can take decades to reach its peak addiction. It creeps up on you so slowly that for the longest time, you have no idea your drinking has become unusual. Because of society's love affair with this drug, you are encouraged to look the other way and ignore the sleight of hand that is really going on.

This is illogical, and at you're the subconscious level, you understand this. The single most influential human need is that of self-preservation. You have no control over this. Your core instinct is to stay alive at all costs. It's hard-wired into every cell in your body. And every one of those cells knows that alcohol is hazardous to you. Your body continually tries to warn you, but you have learned to see those warning signs as positives rather than negatives.

• We may go red in the face or start to sweat, and we lie to ourselves and see it as a sign of merriment.

• We lose our inhibitions (which are there to protect us), and we lie to ourselves that the alcohol has boosted our confidence and self-esteem.

• We drink so much that the brain loses control of our ability to talk, our speech becomes slurred, and yet we still don't see it as a warning that something is wrong.

• Our brains are misfiring so frequently and unpredictably that we can't walk straight and yet we joke about it.

Eventually, we get to the point where our body says enough is enough. It pushes the emergency button that says I must get this poison out of the system, and it forces you to throw up. Do we listen at this point? No. We lie to ourselves that it's the sign of a good night.

Maybe the hangover should be a sign of the damage we did, but no. We have been told over and over again since we were small that a hangover is natural. It's just what happens when you drink. Think about if you got the same feelings the day after you ate a piece of toast, would you even consider eating toast again?

Perhaps you are here reading these words under duress. Maybe a concerned family member, friend, or employer bought this book for you. I can't tell you how many concerned partners I've met who are in relationships with people who resolutely insist they don't have a problem with alcohol. I have yet to meet a single one of these individuals that prove their partner wrong.

Part of *Alcohol Lied to Me* is all about helping you understand how you got to where you are today and why we are all tricked and deceived by alcohol, to understand how this poison is packaged into attractive looking bottles and marketed around the world with multibillion-dollar advertising campaigns. **Alcohol is the ultimate wolf in sheep's clothing,** known to liver consultants and medical professionals around the world (who diligently mop up our mess) as the silent killer. Often before you even know there is a problem, the damage is done.

Free Coaching Video

At the moment, it probably feels like everybody and their dog drinks alcohol. You may be worried about why you appear to be the only one of your friends struggling or even if a sober life is going to be too dull to cope with. If so, make sure you watch my free video:

https://www.stopdrinkingexpert.com/sober-life/

CHAPTER 5:
ALCOHOL – OUR
FAVORITE DRUG

The great relay ~~Staffellauf~~ race of drinking nearly always starts with your parents, and indeed their parents before them, and so on. When you are born into this world, you enter as a completely helpless, weak, and fragile individual driven by the need for love. Strange looking giants surround you, and over time you notice that two of these giants appear to have taken an interest in you. They feed you, care for you, and love you (despite your crying and constant demands on their time).

For many years, these two people have the role of being gods in your eyes. It is utterly inconceivable that they could ever be wrong or would ever lie or mislead you. Their words and actions are your gospel, and before the age of five you blindly accept information from this source without question. Everything you learn and witness at this tender age is stored permanently in your subconscious as a pure fact. In short, what you teach, show, and expose your children to before the age of five will have a significant impact on how they turn out as adults.

Your experience with alcohol started from the moment you entered the world. It's more than likely the giants around you even used this poison to celebrate your arrival into the world. As you watched the giants popping corks out of attractive looking bottles, great smiles grew across their faces, and laughter filled the room. What a fantastic liquid this must be.

How strange that when such a beautiful and unique gift is given

ankündigen

to two happy people, they choose to herald the joyous arrival with a nice glass of a foul-tasting depressant that removes the ability to fully experience the beautiful things going on around us.

Alcohol is a tradition that has been passed down the family line from generation to generation (like a defective gene or biological bad penny). You only need to change the drug to see the truth behind the lies. If a bunch of friends came around to your house to meet your new baby and they all insisted on using cocaine to anoint the baby's head, I am sure you would have something to say.

To further make the point, consider a drug that has only recently become unacceptable. It's not so long back that a fine cigar was mandatory for the menfolk to welcome in a new addition to the family. These days smoking over a newborn child would be seen as the height of irresponsibility.

bescheiden

The story of the humble cigarette is an interesting comparison. Many of my heavy drinking friends would never dream of smoking. They believe it to be an anti-social habit and exceptionally bad for you. Across Europe, these days, every packet of cigarettes comes emblazoned with horrific images of diseased lungs and cancer-infested bodies of smokers. Not long ago, this collective disgust for smoking was not the norm. I grew up in England in the 1970s, a time when smoking was commonplace. Restaurants, theatres and, in fact, all public places were permanently shrouded in a thick fog of cigarette smoke. Candy stores even sold fake, sugar-based cigarettes and cigars so children could pretend to smoke, just like their older family members. Can you imagine the public outrage today if a confectionary company tried to promote their 'training cigarettes' for children?

At the time, this was normal and unquestioned by even the most well-intentioned and intelligent people. Go back a little further and you'll find that cigarettes were marketed as a health-enhancing product, with doctors prescribing them as a cure for various ailments. It took decades for that opinion to change, and even now, the job is still less than only half done.

Go back a little further and you'll find that cigarettes were marketed as a health-enhancing product, with doctors prescribing them as a cure for various ailments. Still, the overriding opinion of western society is that smoking is much worse for you than drinking alcohol. However, according to the World Health Organization's chart of what is most likely to kill us, tobacco use ranks sixth. What surprises most people is alcohol on that very same chart comes in at third, wiping out over 2,500,000 people every year. Not bad going for a harmless social pleasantry!

Let's return to the thought of smoking over a newborn baby in this day and age. I know there will be some objections that it is not a fair comparison. You may object and claim that smoking over a newborn is only dangerous because of the passive smoke you are forcing the baby to inhale. As it is not possible to passively drink, it cannot be reasonably compared to drinking. This is correct in physical terms, but remember, everything you see at this impressionable age is received as a pure fact. From the child's point of view, why would one of the loving giants do something that is dangerous or wrong? Essentially, if their gods drink and it makes them happy, it must be something beautiful. Over the space of a few years, the child will witness many thousands of occasions where pleasure is linked to alcohol: birthday parties, Christmas, Mother's Day, Valentine's Day, and even family BBQs. Repetition is the mother of all learning.

It's the same reason why it's unthinkable to consider throwing a party without having alcoholic drinks. You do it because it's always been done, but if your parents had not passed the poison chalice on to you, and you don't pass it onto your children, the tradition becomes diluted and eventually ineffectual. We don't have to conduct an extravagant experiment over several generations to prove this point. You only need to look at other cultures. Hinduism has many festivals and celebrations that are full of merriment, singing, and dancing without a single drop of alcohol passing anyone's lips.

Alcohol does not make a party – people do! But just try throwing a party in your part of the world without any alcohol and half your guests will leave and go to the nearest pub. It's not that drinking creates fun; it's that people who are out of control of their drinking are miserable without alcohol and can't think about anything else when they are without it. This isn't the fault of your party; it's the fault of a society that teaches every one of us how to get addicted to a powerful and deceptive drug

verschlimmert

and then compounds the problem by making us believe that it's normal.

Most people who drink wine every day claim they honestly like the taste of it. This is nonsense. Alcohol tastes so bad that the drink manufacturers essentially have to find increasingly potent ways to cover it up. The body is an amazing and sophisticated piece of natural engineering. Despite what lies you have taught yourself on a superficial level, you still cannot break the rules your body has created over millions of years of evolution. Right at the top of our hierarchy of needs is the need to protect life, to stay alive at all costs. This is hardwired into every cell, every molecule, and every tiny atom of your being. You can't decide to stop your heart beating or never to breathe again. You can't, because it breaks the ultimate built-in rule, that of ensuring self-preservation at all costs.

The reason pure alcohol tastes bad is the same reason rotting meat or moldy, fungus-infested bread tastes bad. Your body is warning you that you are consuming something that is putting you at risk. Think about it — in a hospital operating theatre, the room and the entire medical team that works in it must be 100% free of germs, bacteria, and viral contaminants. So what do they scrub their hands with? Not soap, but alcohol. Because it instantly kills any living organism upon contact! It pulls every bit of moisture out of their cells and causes them to self-implode. At a microcellular level, alcohol is akin to thermo-nuclear war; nothing survives. Do you honestly believe you have some fantastic internal system to get around this fact? Somehow, when you consume this dangerous disinfectant, it doesn't do less damage just because you have hidden it in a bit of cranberry juice.

Alcohol tastes horrible. You already know this but have forgotten, or as is more accurate, you have conditioned yourself to believe the opposite. As a hypnotherapist, I can tell you that this is entirely possible and can be easily replicated in a relatively short amount of time to prove the point. In hypnosis, the conscious (thinking and judging) mind is bypassed, which means I can speak directly to the subconscious and implant beliefs without interference from the ego. Obviously, in therapy or in the hypnosis tracks that I have created, all suggestions are positive and delivered for your benefit. However, it is entirely possible for me to condition you to enjoy something deeply unpleasant, such as a hard punch on the arm! If, while under hypnosis, I hit you hard but told you it felt amazing and repeated that process many times and over several sessions, you would eventually begin to crave the experience.

You can see this feature of the human mind demonstrated in the most horrendous situations. When people are held captive by a sole individual, despite the fact that this person has abducted, tortured, and abused them, the victim slowly, over time, begins to develop feelings for the perpetrator. Despite suffering at the hands of this person, they become conditioned to their environment and begin to want to please the person who holds them against their will. This phenomenon has been studied at length by eminent psychologists and is known as 'Stockholm syndrome.'

To a certain degree, I believe you are suffering from a form of this syndrome. Alcohol has abused you for so long that you now firmly think there is a benefit to you. You have fallen in love with a killer!

I say again, alcohol tastes bad; your first interaction with it proved that point. When you first sneaked a drink of your father's neat whiskey, did it taste amazing, or did it taste vile? Most people will say it tasted disgusting, and they couldn't imagine getting hooked on something that tasted that bad. The taste of alcohol has not changed, so the only explanation for your current belief that it tastes good is that you have changed. You have conditioned yourself to believe alcohol tastes good. Don't feel badly; you have had a significant helping hand from society and the advertising industry.

What you must understand from this point on is that what you previously believed about alcohol was a lie and nothing more. If I poured a glass of pure alcohol and asked you to dip your little finger in and taste it, I am sure you will agree it tastes horrible. Indeed, if you drank that glass of liquid, you would shortly be dead. Funny really, because since birth, you have been programmed to ignore this and instead believe that alcohol is natural and an everyday part of life that you must consume if you are to be considered fun and a member of the gang by your peers. This is a throwback to our primitive evolution. We are still pack animals to a certain extent, and this is another reason for our global addiction to this drug.

The second reason is best explained by a smarter man than I, a famous psychologist called Abraham Maslow. Maslow is known for establishing the theory of a hierarchy of needs, writing that human beings are motivated by unsatisfied needs and that specific lower needs need to be satisfied before higher needs can be.

Although there is a continuous cycle of wars, murder, and deceit, he believed that human beings are not innately violent. Violence and other evils occur when human needs are thwarted. In other words, people who are deprived of lower needs, such as safety, may defend themselves by violent means. He did not believe that humans are violent because they enjoy violence, or that they lie, cheat, and steal because they enjoy doing it.

According to Maslow, there are general types of needs (physiological, safety, love, and esteem), and they must be satisfied before a person can act unselfishly. He called these needs 'deficiency needs.' As long as we are motivated to satisfy these needs, we are moving toward growth, toward self-actualization.

Satisfying needs is healthy, and blocking gratification makes us sick and unhappy. In other words, we are all 'needs junkies' with cravings that must and should be satisfied. If we don't concentrate on doing this, we will become sick. Willpower is an illusionary weapon created by the egoic mind. It's like your enemy giving you a plastic sword and saying 'Here, use this to protect yourself if I ever attack you!.' This is exactly why people have such a hard time trying to go cold turkey with their drinking. One morning you wake up and say, 'That's it! I am never drinking again.' By lunchtime, you have a psychological itch so intense you are almost screaming inside.

Willpower does not work because it forces your subconscious and conscious mind into civil war. It's the same reason why the moment you go on a diet you become hungrier than you thought possible.

Here is the secret to stopping drinking: you need to attach more pleasure to not drinking than there is to drinking. You have to remove the need by understanding the truth about alcohol. It is not a social pleasantry, but rather an attractively packaged

poison. A multi-billion dollar marketing campaign for the alcoholic drinks industry is working exceptionally hard to convince you otherwise, but you have to trust your gut on this one.

Let me put the point another way. I have two wonderful children whom I love and adore more than life itself. Maybe you also have children, and you can understand my love and need to protect my children from the harms of the world. Let me ask you a question: If you had some strong rat poison for dealing with a tricky vermin infestation, would you keep it in a chocolate box and put it within reach of your kids?

Alcohol is similar to an anti-personnel landmine. You step on it, and beyond a small clunk, all appears fine ... until you try and step off it. Then, and only then, you discover what a mess you are really in.

Our desire to drink is what we call a 'proponent need', a need that has a powerful influence over our actions. Everyone has proponent needs, but those needs will vary among individuals. A teenager may need to feel that they are accepted by a group. A heroin addict will need to satisfy their cravings for heroin to function normally in society, and because of the strength of the need, they are unlikely to worry about acceptance by other people.

There is no difference between alcohol and heroin or alcohol and nicotine. The only difference is that drinking is socially acceptable. But ask yourself this, if it had not yet been invented and I brought it to market tomorrow, do you think I would get it even halfway through the rigorous testing process modern-day food and beverages have to go through?

Around the world, there is a very popular television program called 'Dragon's Den,' where would-be entrepreneurs pitch their ideas to already successful venture capitalists seeking investment. Can you imagine taking your fabulous new drink additive called alcohol before the Dragons and asking them to invest? The conversation might go something like this:

Entrepreneur: Hello, Dragon. I am here to ask for $1,000,000,000 to launch my new drink supplement called alcohol. Would you like to try a glass?

A small sample of the product is poured into shot glasses for each of the investors in turn. Cautiously, they take a sip.

Dragons: My God, that tastes disgusting!

Entrepreneur: Yes, it does initially, but we have tested it quite extensively and find that people do eventually become accustomed to the taste. Plus, we use sweet-tasting carrier beverages such as orange juice and cola to cover up the real taste. When they get used to it, the consumer will feel amazing! Parties go with a bang, everything seems funnier, and there is a massive euphoric sense of well-being.

Dragons: Sounds interesting. Are there any downsides to this new drink?

Entrepreneur: Erm, well, there is a slight risk of vomiting, sexually transmitted disease from unprotected sex, not to mention the violence and serious damage to careers, reputations, and relationships. You probably need to be aware that several millions of our potential customers will have to die in agony from organ failure. Apart from that, I think this product has great potential.

Dragons: I am not investing in that! I am out!

Am I going to ridiculous extremes to make my point here? Perhaps. But no more ridiculous than people around the western world claiming that the disgusting liquid they took a sneaky drink of as a kid when their parents weren't looking has somehow turned into an exquisite and delicious beverage. The alcohol tastes just as vile as it ever did, but you have allowed this attractively packaged poison to fit you with some very impressive rose-tinted glasses!

Here's an experiment for you — wait until Friday evening and go check your friends out on Facebook. You will see status after status along these lines:

Wine O-Clock... I think so.

Friday night and I can hear the beer monster calling.

Friday night takeaway and a bottle of wine... it would be rude not to.

Thank God it's the weekend, chilling out with a nice bottle of red.

Enjoying a very large glass of wine... I love the weekends.

Cheeky glass of wine on the go.

That last one particularly amuses me, that we could explain

away what we are doing by adding a cute descriptive term before admitting the truth. You wouldn't hear this with any other drug, would you? Imagine if we talked about heroin in the same way.

'Friday night, a cheeky hit of heroin... it would be rude not to.'

It's time to grow up and realize you have been scammed. Yes, you. The bright and worldly-wise individual who has a good job and a successful career. The very same person who achieved all that success, has been fooled by the oldest trick in the book.

You have become addicted to a drug, and this has created a recurring psychological itch that makes you want to scratch it at regular intervals. You have created a deficiency need, and according to Abraham Maslow, when the deficiency needs are met, instantly, other, and higher needs emerge, and these, rather than physiological hunger, dominate the person. And when these, in turn, are satisfied, again new (and still higher) needs emerge, and so on. As one desire is satisfied, another pops up to take its place. It is this automatic behavior pattern that means we never really get the motivation to focus on what needs we are serving. The ego once again complicates the matter by insisting on more — more gratification, more consumption, more love, more power, just more!

We are complicated beings, and our addiction to alcohol is just one cog in an intricate and needy machine. We are also addicted to love and significance, which distracts our attention from the dependence we could actually do something about! Humans have a desire to belong to groups: clubs, workgroups, religious groups, families, gangs, etc. We need to feel loved by others, not necessarily in a sexual way. I suppose another way of putting it would be to say that we need to feel significant. We need to be accepted by others. Performers appreciate applause. We need to be needed. Beer commercials, in addition to playing on our desire for sex, also often show how beer makes for camaraderie. When was the last time you saw a beer commercial with someone drinking beer alone?

But does alcohol really answer the social need within us? We like to get together and consume this drug, but does it really create a sensation of love?

Ask yourself how you would feel about ordering a drink of alcohol in a room full of teetotalers. Perhaps group drinking creates a sensation of safety in numbers; it makes us feel like what we are doing is perfectly acceptable in the eyes of our peers. Plus, we also get to witness people who are 'far more drunk' than we are!

Though alcohol is touted as the social drug, it actually turns us into very anti-social individuals. We become loud and opinionated. In some cases, it makes us aggressive and violent. Even the 'happy drunks' slur and talk nothing but pure gibberish as they fall over even the most obvious obstacle. Uncontrolled laughter, loss of bladder control, vomiting in the streets and in the back of taxi cabs are just a few of the accepted norms of this most social of drugs.

When you stop drinking, you will look at all this universally endorsed chaos and see it for what it really is: group insanity on a global level.

Free Coaching Video

Be honest. Are you drinking to cover up a bigger problem? Often alcohol is not really the issue; it's just a symptom of a bigger problem. A lot of people are using alcohol to cope with emotional pain, loneliness, a broken marriage, and so on.

Alcohol is our favorite drug to deal with the stresses of modern life, but does it really do what it says on the tin? If you're interested in exploring how you might be using alcohol to avoid reality, watch my video:

https://www.stopdrinkingexpert.com/mailer-reality/

CHAPTER 6: LIE DOWN WITH DOGS – GET UP WITH FLEAS

Another reason why quitting drinking using willpower is so tricky is that the social deck of cards is not stacked in your favor. Every part of aspirational western life is geared towards alcohol being a part of your overall success. If you become fabulously wealthy, one of the things you simply must have in your mansion in the country is a well-stocked cellar full of the most elegant wines from around the world.

Recently in the UK, a group of bankers was highly publicized for spending $51,000 on fine wine over the course of a single meal. The marketing machine behind alcohol is so much more devious and calculating than the one behind cigarettes ever was. Not only would they have you believe that wine is good for you, but they also suggest you are nobody unless you own the most expensive versions of their poison.

Let's take a look at champagne, essentially fizzy white wine grown in an ever-expanding region of France. It ranges in price from $20 per bottle to many thousands of dollars a bottle. Even this overpriced, attractively packed plonk has its own inner circle of snobbery. I have been to media parties where guests have turned their nose up at a $30 bottle of champagne and demanded better quality Cristal or Krug, costing upwards of $450 a bottle. These people are not more refined, of a higher class, or more educated than anyone else They are just examples of individuals who have fallen for the most significant scam going but are using snobbery to cover it up.

In my book *The Hypnotic Salesman,* I talk about the two most potent motivational forces in the world. They are the law of scarcity and the law of social proof.

Scarcity is the most potent form of leverage there is. It is the reason why we will pay vast sums of money for rare diamonds and one-off pieces of fine art. Objects that are in limited supply are attractive to our ego. Owning these things give us a sense of being essential and make us feel special.

The next significant determining pressure is the law of social proof. In 1968, the social psychiatrists Stanley Milgram, Leonard Bickman, and Lawrence Berkowitz made a decision to bring about a little trouble. To begin with, they put an individual man on a street intersection and had him look up at a vacant sky for sixty seconds.

A small portion of the passing pedestrians stopped to check out what the man was looking at, but the majority simply strolled past. The next time around, the psychiatrists placed five skyward-looking guys on the intersection. This time, four times as many people stopped to stare at the empty sky.

When the psychiatrists placed 14 individuals on the intersection, 45% percent of all passers-by stopped. Raising the cohort of onlookers yet again made more than 80% percent of people passing by turn their heads and look up.

This research study seems, at an initial glance, to be one more illustration of folks' desire to conform. However, it highlights the concept of 'social proof,' which is the propensity to think that if a considerable number of other people are doing something or strongly believe something, there must be a valid explanation why. This is separate from congruity. Folks are not looking up at the heavens due to peer pressure or from worry about being criticized. They're looking up at the wild blue yonder because they presume, pretty logically, that loads of men and women would not be staring skyward if there weren't something to watch. That's why the group ends up being more dominant as it becomes larger; every extra man or woman is verification that something significant is taking place. The controlling belief appears to be that when matters are unclear, the very best thing to do is just follow along.

Social proof used to support cigarette smoking as a reasonable habit. Virtually everybody was doing it, and for that reason, the tacit viewpoint was that it must be a beneficial thing to do. As cigarette smoking restrictions come into power in increasingly more locations, this social legislation is being disrupted, and because of this, the practice is dropping off. However, with drinking, this potent kind of leverage is still significantly at play. When I go into a bar or pub and ask for a soda, the folks who don't know me and have no idea what I do for a living frantically need to know what's wrong and the reason that I am not drinking alcohol. When I tell them that I do not drink, their reaction resembles what I envision people get when they reveal they have something incurable. Their faces are flooded with extreme sadness and sympathy, and they say things like 'Oh, how awful for you.' It's a strange situation to get used to, but it is all a component of the group madness that drinking creates.

Battling the desire to consume alcohol when the law of social proof supports that it is a beneficial practice is like attempting to arm-wrestle an angry gorilla. If your existing social network includes an array of people who drink, trust me when I say, they do not want you to stop drinking. Why? Evidently, these people care about you and want you to succeed in hitting your personal goals and targets in life? Surely these friends understand you are taking a brave and challenging step towards better health and ensuring you will be around to see your children, and eventually their children grow up?

Ungeachtet
Despite what these people feel about you, no matter how much love and empathy they have for you, they are still blinded by their own addiction. Remember, 80% of people who drink are no longer in control. Granted, all who drink on at different points along the path, but all are on the same road. All drinkers are sitting in the same mousetrap, stuffing their cheeks with cheese under the illusion that they are in control. In reality, the trap is in control and always was.

Human beings are motivated by two distinct needs: the need to avoid pain and the need to gain pleasure. I will go into much more detail about this later in this book, but for now, I will offer a simple explanation. If you introduce pain into someone's life, they will subconsciously do absolutely everything possible to restore the balance. This does not necessarily mean that they will continue the forward momentum until they reach the point of experiencing pleasure. Usually, just going far enough to stop the pain is enough.

Deep down inside, we all know that alcohol is terrible for us. All the signs are there; we choose to ignore them. So when you stop drinking, you appear to raise your standards above those of the people around you. As you raise your own standards, you automatically highlight their low standards, and this causes psychological pain to everyone around you.

I can demonstrate this quite easily — simply go to a party where drinks are flowing and announce that you are going to drink water all night. I guarantee at least three or more guests will pounce on you like vampires in the blood bank. Watch how desperate they become for you to have a drink. They throw lines at you like, 'Just have one little one.,' and, 'Come on. Lighten up. You only live once.' If you are male, they may even question your sexuality. WHY? Why do well-meaning, kind-hearted individuals suddenly turn into schoolyard bullies when you stop drinking?

The answer is simple: They don't want you to remind them that what they are doing must one day also stop. Whether by choice or by a different, somewhat more unfortunate set of circumstances, it's easier for them to remove the pain (i.e., you and the highlight placed upon their own weakness) than address their own problem in the first place, and human beings will almost always take the path of least resistance.

So, for this section, I will remind you that if you lie down with dogs, you WILL get up with fleas. The next time you are in a pub, and someone asks you if you want a drink and you reply 'no' because you are not thirsty, remember, as they laugh, throw insults, and coax you into reconsidering your blatant faux pas, that you are the one on the higher ground looking down, not the other way around. They may be laughing and smiling as they point out your foolish error, but make no mistake, their need for you to drink is not for your benefit; it's purely to remove pain from their own situation.

Before I emigrated from the UK to Cyprus, I tried to get a head start on my move to a foreign country by taking Greek lessons with a fantastic teacher called Linda Weaver from Warrington. Linda spent nearly 20 years living in Greece and even married a Greek man during her time there. She has a superb grasp of the language and is an accomplished and famous teacher of the subject. However, no matter how many lessons I had, I could not get my head around the complexities of the native tongue of Cyprus, my future home. I believe the main reason I struggled is that my exposure to Greek was limited to the one hour a week I spent in Linda's conservatory having my lesson. Once I left her pretty suburban home, I never heard another word of Greek until I arrived back on the same driveway a week or so later.

However, this embarrassingly remedial ability in the Greek language only seemed to apply when I was in the UK. Once in Cyprus, I picked up phrases and vocabulary at a spectacular rate. After just a few weeks of residency, I could have basic conversations with most people I came into contact with. Does being surrounded by the very things you aspire to be really make that much of an impact?

The answer is a massive 'Yes!' It is the human ability to adapt that is as much the reason for our success as a species as it is an explanation for our failings. Put an Englishman in a foreign country and, eventually, he will become a local, absorbing the cultural differences and making them a part of his personality. Unfortunately, we are just as good as adapting to damaging and dangerous situations as we are to the positive behaviors around us. While the human body does not want to live in an environment where its host regularly consumes an addictive poison, it will still adapt to this lifestyle out of pure determination to survive and thrive.

If you are in an environment surrounded by drinkers, you will find this whole process slightly more difficult. Smokers who live with a partner who also smokes will find it more difficult to quit than someone who lives in a smoke-free home. There is nothing you can do about other people, so forget about trying to change them. Please do not even try to preach this message to your friends and colleagues. They don't want to hear it. The best counterbalance to this problem is to also socialize in an environment of like-minded people. Hang out with other individuals who have also recognized the truth about alcohol and are starting out on a sober lifestyle.

You might think it strange that I tell you not to preach this message to other people. After all, I am an author, and I make my living from the royalties from book sales, so why would I try and persuade you to keep this method a secret?

Drinking alcohol is so firmly embedded into our collective consciousness that when you stop drinking for good, you will observe some bizarre situations. As I am writing this, one of those occasions has just conveniently arisen. I am typing this section of *Alcohol Lied to Me* 37,000 feet over the French Alps en route from Manchester, England to Larnaca, Cyprus. As I boarded and took my seat, a familiar face greeted me. It was Andrea, a friend of mine whom I have not seen for many years and now works for the airline. She just happens to be the senior cabin stewardess aboard this flight to Cyprus. It made me feel quite special to get a hug and kiss on the cheek from the air hostess as she took my ticket. That has certainly never happened before. As she hugged me, she whispered in my ear, 'Don't worry; I will make sure you are looked after.'

There was no room in first class, but she made sure I got special attention, I am sure to the annoyance of the other passengers seated nearby. I was moved to sit with a whole row of seats to myself, and not more than 30 minutes into the flight, her colleague approached me and asked if I would like a complimentary drink. I ordered a coffee. The same stewardess came back an hour later and asked if I would like something else. I ordered fresh orange juice and some crisps, which she quickly and politely delivered to my seat with a smile. Not long after, Andrea came to see me herself, and with a confused expression on her face, asked, 'Do you not want some wine or whiskey?' I assured her I was fine, and she smiled at me as she dashed off to respond to another passenger who had pressed the call button.

About a third of the way through this five-hour flight, I had already enjoyed a coffee, orange juice, mineral water, a hot meal, and now a cola, all gratis, thanks to my friend, Andrea.

But something was wrong. Andrea sat in the empty seat next to me. 'Are you sure you don't want some wine?' she asked, and again I smiled back at her and said, 'I am fine.' Her face crumpled with confusion. 'Are you driving as soon as you land, is that why you don't want it? You can take some bottles with you if you want.' I held a hand up to emphasize the point subconsciously and smiled again. 'No, Andrea, honestly, I am fine. I don't need any wine.' She nodded, smiled, and walked back down the cabin, obviously perplexed by the strange man who didn't leap at the chance for free alcohol. As she walked away, I got the distinct impression I had offended her somehow. It couldn't have been because I had refused her generosity because I had eaten and drank like a king for the first three hours of the flight and not paid a penny for the privilege.

In a society where 80% of people drink poison for apparently social reasons, this is the sort of event you will experience over and over again, especially when alcohol is offered free.

Turning down free poison appears to be one of the most offensive things you can do in polite society. This simple act seems to cause significant discomfort and distrust for the person offering the alcohol. When you ask for a soft drink instead, they assure you that it isn't a problem, and yet they walk off to the fridge with the most disingenuous expression on their face you have ever seen.

How do you explain your sober lifestyle choice?

My advice to you is – simply don't. You are not the one doing something wrong. I have found it is best just to avoid getting into explanations or reasons why you don't want alcohol. Don't feel the urge to churn out the old stalwart of, 'I am on antibiotics,' because that just moves the interrogation a little further down the road. At some point, you are going to find yourself in another social situation with the same person. The fact that you are considered the strange one because you don't want to ingest toxin is clear evidence of how twisted the collective thinking of society has become around this drug. In reality, they should be explaining to you why they want to drink an addictive drug.

In all social situations around alcohol, firmly but politely turn down alcohol. You don't need to explain why you are not drinking; there is no need to make statements about being a tee-totaler. You should never force your views about alcohol on other people. Honestly, this is a fruitless pursuit and a complete waste of time. It would be easier for you to sell double glazing to a man who lives in a tent. They simply don't want to buy what you are selling!

A friend of mine once told me that he doesn't trust people who don't drink! That is seriously impressive brainwashing you are witnessing there. Mr. Alcohol, stand up and take a bow. You have managed to program 80% of the western world to believe it's the people who don't drink poison for fun who are the ones with questionable judgment. If it weren't so sad, it should be con-sidered manipulation psychology approaching degrees of pure genius. Imagine if McDonald's could come up with a marketing campaign that worked so effectively that society went on to be-lieve that it's the obese people who are not eating enough fast food!

If you are looking for a great way to find new sober friends, there is a great, free social networking site designed just for that purpose. *Sober And Out* lets you meet likeminded people from around the world and in your town or city. It's a great way to meet people who don't want to make the center of everything alcohol. You can find out more and sign up to this free service at www.SoberAndOut.com.

CHAPTER 7:
THRESHOLD
MOMENTS

Let's talk more about motivation and the theory that we are all enslaved to two basic driving desires: the need to avoid pain and gain pleasure. Everything in your life, at one level or another, is based on how it relates to these two primary needs. An easy example to illustrate this point is to ask you to take a good look at your body now. It's unlikely there isn't something about it you don't like or think could be improved. After all, we are all our own worst critics, and whether it's the general shape or size of your body, or there are more specific areas you are not comfortable with, there will undoubtedly be some areas which you would like to improve.

So the big question is, why don't you do something about it?

Why don't overweight people who are painfully unhappy with their size and shape, correct the problem? Why don't people who get out of breath running up a flight of stairs start an exercise program to improve their fitness? The answer is that they have an internal belief that the application of the cure creates more pain than the eventual pleasure of succeeding in the goal.

Imagine an overweight individual who hates what they see when they look in the mirror, who gets depressed while clothes shopping because they struggle to find the designer clothes they want in their size. Can we agree that for that person slimming down and becoming the trim, fit, and athletic person they dream of would be an amazing feeling?

It would bring enormous pleasure to anyone to be able to walk down the street and notice the admiring glances of passersby, to make any clothes look fantastic on their chiseled and defined torso. Surely such pleasure is worth the pain of dieting? Judging by the escalating levels of chronic obesity, this does not appear to be the case.

In reality, human beings will do significantly more to avoid pain than they will do to gain pleasure. While it's undoubtedly true, having a supermodel body would bring great pleasure, the perceived journey to get there contains too much pain for most people to contemplate tolerating. So the result is that many people remain in perpetual limbo with most things in their life that they are not satisfied with. They are not happy with the amount of money they earn but prefer to hang in a mediocre position than suffer the initial pain of pushing through their comfort zone to become a more skilled, talented, and experienced, or specialist employee. How many people remain in a dead-end job, daydreaming of starting their own business, but NEVER do anything about it?

The same rule applies to alcohol. You know deep down inside that you would be happier without poison flushing around in your system on a daily basis. You know you would have more money in your pocket, more time awake, and less time crashed out in a drunken paralysis. You know how wonderful it would feel not to care if you have a drink today or not, so why don't you deal with it? Simple — because at the moment, you associate more pain with removing alcohol than you associate pleasure with stopping drinking.

Because of the ever-changing needs and demands of the ego, this perception of what constitutes pleasure and pain is always shifting. The most likely reason that you purchased this book is that you encountered what I call a 'threshold moment.' Essentially, something happened that temporally altered the balance of the scales. This is an event so traumatic that it causes an unbearable amount of pain that sends you into a massive, determined period of change. Let me give you a few examples of threshold moments in relation to drinking before I give you my own:

Life is cruising along nicely in your usual blinkered and ironic state, where you are acutely aware that you are drinking far too much and probably doing serious damage to your health, career, and loved ones, and yet you still reach for the bottle of wine every night as soon as you get home, happy to ignore all the warning signs in favor of blind ignorance.

One night, you are sitting watching television, your ego sedated and comfortably numb by the glass of mild anesthetic grasped comfortably in your hand. Your five-year-old daughter comes up to you with a carefully and proudly drawn picture. It's a colorful drawing of you, her daddy. You are slumped in front of the television and in your hand a bottle of wine! BANG! Suddenly it hits you like a tonne of bricks – this is how your child sees you. Through her pure, innocent eyes, she sees you for the real addict that you are. Children have no binding compulsion to pull any punches or to spare your feelings; they just tell it how it is.

Children are blank canvasses, and they learn in their formative years solely by watching us, the grown-ups. This social pleasantry that has made us so utterly miserable is here now because it has been passed down through the generations as a curse wrapped up in shiny paper and labeled as a gift.

The reason this book gets updated annually is that every year, thousands more people use it to help them stop drinking. Many of them send me their stories, and the collective wisdom of all us ex-drinkers is worth more than the sum of their parts.

This is a heartbreaking story I was emailed only this week from Linda (not her real name as she has asked to remain anonymous). Linda grew up with an alcoholic mother and later went on to have her struggle with drink until she joined my online club last year. If you are a parent and wonder how your drinking affects your children, Linda's story is difficult but vital for you to read:

> Being brought up by my alcoholic mother has had a profound effect on my self-perception and my relationship with alcohol.
>
> My childhood is a combination of good vs. bad, but alcohol made the world around me evil. I was protected from nothing and exposed to all as a result of having no parents to shelter me. Alcohol made my childhood a living nightmare. It took away the amazing, loving, proud mother I had, and gave me a woman that I was mortified to be associated with.
>
> I remember seeing her tears, her worries, over money, anxiety in social situations, and what was the answer? Alcohol. That was her answer each time, no matter the devastation caused by the last binge. She was so embroiled in the vicious pattern that she couldn't be a mother. I grew up being able to do whatever I wanted, and there were no consequences for my actions as my mum was a drunk. She would turn up drunk to formal meetings with my principal but then forget the conversation, so I got away with everything. This all accumulated into a general lack of respect I had for anyone, even myself. I respected no one and listened to no one. No one cared for me. After all, if your parents can't be there for you, who can? More than a lack of respect for others, I didn't respect or love myself. My mother never took time to emotionally invest in me, which left me feeling unworthy of love, so I rebelled to get

the attention I craved.

My mother's drinking took her away from me. She didn't see the child I was; she didn't acknowledge my achievements, and she didn't attend my sporting events, all because alcohol got in the way. I was dragged up in a world no child should have to witness.

When she wasn't drinking she was the mum I loved and the best mother on planet earth. She would apologize, have a movie day, buy us sweets, and tell us it would never happen again, but the pattern continued.

As a result of my upbringing, I went through a decade of my life unable to have a few drinks with my friends. I went from entering the bar to being paralytic as I had no control over my drinks. The way I was brought up is that you drink until you're unconscious; there is no middle ground. It took years to bring this behavior under control, and even now, alcohol scares me.

I lost my childhood and so much more because of my mother's addiction to alcohol. I would not wish any child to experience the life I did with my mum.

Regardless of the world she brought me up in, I still love her as I know somewhere inside she is still there — but alcohol has won this battle, I only hope it won't win the war too!

Linda, United Kingdom

Whether you have your own child's super honest portrait of you pinned to the refrigerator door or perhaps Linda's story made you question your behavior, these sorts of events can be considered for many to be what I call a threshold moment — an event so powerfully painful that it forces you to change. The 'pain vs. pleasure' scales take a dramatic nudge in one direction, and your perception of what you are doing changes enough for you to take action. Normally people on the road to giving up attractively packaged poison have several increasingly severe threshold moments along the way.

Let me tell you what my personal threshold moment was like:

I am wonderfully blessed, and it could be said I have been guilty in the past of not appreciating that fact. I could be accused of being fantastically blasé about my two beautiful children who are 11 and 7. Without a modicum of ego here, I can tell you they look at me like I am faultless. I could have lived up to that view much better without alcohol distracting me from the true beauty of the gift I had been consecrated with.

I can't tell you how many fun days were missed, just because I could not see a way for the day to include alcohol. I don't want to torture myself by considering how many options I took purely because they included alcohol. Option A might have been more fun for my children and option C might have been more enjoyable for my wife, but if option B included alcohol, then that was always the only choice I made because I couldn't see how anything could be enjoyed without a drink.

At this point, I will remind you that while I am sharing this with you, I don't believe in beating yourself up with your mistakes of the past. The past is very important because it brought you to where you are now, but it has absolutely no relevance on tomorrow. Just because I made bad decisions in the past does not mean I am compelled to make them again now, tomorrow, or at any point in the future. Every dawn brings an exciting new opportunity for you to get it right. Trust me, I know you are at the start of a tough journey, but the commitment you have made just investing your money in this book (money you could quite have easily spent on your favorite brand of alcohol) is a dramatic and profound statement of intent.

Remember, as Woody Allen says, '80% of success is just turning up,' so if you are here as the result of a painful threshold moment, don't let that pain subside enough for you to believe that purchasing this book is enough to make a difference. Absorb it over and over. Use the subliminal tools available from my website to help you alter your programming around alcohol.

Every time you observe the ego and catch it in the act of attempting to take over control of your choices, you reduce its power by a fraction of one percent. If you consistently keep doing this over time, I know the future is bright. Every day is worth living, and if you don't believe me about that right here and now, just try missing one of them!

When I became a dad, I was determined to be closer to my children than my dad was with me. I would always be there; I would be the kind of dad that they could always turn to no matter what. I would be the father who took his son fishing and his daughter to see the latest pop concert. My children and my wife would be safe, secure, and happy. They would never have to worry about bills, or whether we could afford this or that. I would work as hard as I needed just to make it happen. What I never considered in this grand plan was what would happen if you took *me* out of the equation. What if I was not around to provide for and protect my family? In 1997 I had to consider that the situation could be a very real and likely possibility.

At this point, I was drinking in the region of two bottles of wine a day. Of course, I was still vehemently lying to myself. I figured that because I had no urge to drink first thing in the morning, and my drinking in no way affected my work, I could not be an alcoholic. If I am honest, I didn't and still don't like the word alcoholic. For me, it describes the guy lying in the gutter swilling cheap whiskey from a brown paper bag, not me. I could not possibly have a serious drink problem; I was a Director of two companies and had just been appointed to the board of a children's charity.

And yet every evening as soon as I got home, I opened the first bottle of wine and gulped the first half down like it was the first gasp of oxygen to a free diver returning from the depths of the deep blue. By the time I fell into bed, the second bottle would be empty; perhaps I would throw away the last mouthful just so if my wife asked I would honestly say that I had not had a full two bottles of wine.

I consider myself to be a relatively intelligent person, and yet here I was, throwing a mouthful of wine away so that I could face my spouse and lie with a free conscience. It's amazing how tunnel-visioned we become, how we ignore the unnatural behavior we should recognize as warning signs.

At the height of my problem, I couldn't even contemplate a night at the movies without a drink. Movie theatres are full of popcorn, sweets, and super-sized buckets of fizzy drinks, but rarely can you take an alcoholic drink into the movie. This was a problem for me (although it seemed normal at the time). After a hard day at work, I didn't think it was fair that I should be deprived of my evening drink by a movie. I would sometimes buy a quarter bottle of whiskey and pour it into one of those enormous colas and sip on it all the way through the film.

Once alcohol takes hold of you, it never lets go. The grip is always tightened. I can't remember when I started drinking in movie theatres, but it didn't phase me. Alcohol moves so slowly that you don't even notice how deep you are sinking. I hope you stay with me to the end of the book. But regardless, please never assume your situation will get better on its own. If you ignore the problem now, it can only get worse.

This was my threshold moment!

In January 1997, after a particularly heavy festive season, I started to get a dull ache in my right abdomen just under my right rib. I dismissed it as one of a hundred different minor, insignificant medical problems, from a bit of food poisoning to intolerance of wheat. I even considered paying $400 for a food allergy blood test. In summary, I considered everything apart from the obvious, that the 140 units of alcohol a week were destroying my insides the same way alcohol destroys all life at a cellular level.

By February, the dull ache was preventing me from getting to sleep, and I started researching my symptoms on the Internet. As I scanned the possible reasons for pain in this region, I suddenly became genuinely scared. Website after website suggested liver cancer, liver failure, liver cirrhosis, pancreatic failure, alcohol-induced gall bladder disease. The lists went on and on, all horrific illnesses, all caused by alcohol, and many were irreversible. I made an appointment to see my doctor.

In my lifetime, I have never had anything seriously wrong with me; I have only ever been to the doctor for a cold or simple chest infection. My past experiences with the medical profession meant I always confidently expect to be told that the condition will clear up on its own, or that a short dose of antibiotics would be all that is needed. This time was different.

I sat in the doctor's waiting room, shaking with fear. I walked in and explained my symptoms. He asked how much I was drinking. I lied and said I used to drink a lot, but now I have no more than a glass of wine a night. Can you believe that even at this point, I still lied? Of course, you can — you still do it all the time! This is the power of this drug. In honest fear for my life, face to face with a medical professional who was there to help me, I still lied to protect my opportunity to drink. Despite the fact that it was slowly killing me, I couldn't cope with the possibility that it would be taken away from me, so I lied to the doctor.

If you are not from the UK, let me explain that doctors in England are normally seen at the cost of the state on the National Health Service. Surgeries are usually over-prescribed, and getting an appointment is sometimes difficult. My allocated time with Dr. White was just five minutes; behind me there were another seven patients, all waiting for their own five minutes. After 35 minutes of examinations and questions, I knew this was going to be a very different experience than I was used to.

I still expected, even after all the fuss, for the doctor to nod reassuringly and say, 'Well, I've checked you over, and you seem fine. Come back in a month if it doesn't improve.' Dr. White had a concerned but kind face; he looked up from his notes over his small round glasses and said, 'There is a very real possibility there is something serious behind your pain. I don't have the facilities here for examining you to the level I need to, so I am having you sent to the gastroenterology department at the hospital.'

Hospital! Surely not! That is where sick people go. The health service is overextended as it is. Surely they wouldn't waste a valuable bed on someone young and healthy like me. As I walked home, neither cured nor reassured, this was the point when I realized this was not a figment of my imagination. I had possibly seriously damaged my body by selfishly drinking my attractively packaged poison.

I sat at home and watched my children play and it felt like my heart had been ripped out. Knowing how much I love my family, how could I do that to them? How could I leave my children without a daddy? How could I be so selfish that I would make my children go through the pain of watching their dad's funeral? How could I be so pathetic that I would risk making my wife a single parent with two devastated children to look after and no income? I am not ashamed to tell you, my world was ripped apart that evening and I cried myself to sleep in a world of self-pity, regret, and guilt.

This was my ultimate threshold moment; it altered the balance of all things. For a brief time, the pain of continuing to drink was greater than the pain of living without my drug. I stopped drinking for eight weeks, and the pain subsided a little. The hospital performed dozens of blood tests and scans, and I was awaiting a liver biopsy because my enzymes were all over the place (a clear indication that my liver was in trauma). The problem with relying on a threshold event to cure your problem is, as soon as the pain generated by the threshold begins to fade, your determination to stick to your goals fades too, and you're back in the hands of good old-fashioned willpower. Let me tell you here and now, willpower is no friend of yours or mine.

Willpower is a civil war because it breaks a human need rule; it breaks the law of scarcity. if you want proof that you are fighting a losing battle trying to stop drinking with willpower, let me prove it to you.

The classic self-help process that relies on willpower is dieting. When you look in the mirror and decide you need to shed some weight, as soon as you start restricting the amount of food you are allowed, the body goes into shock. Suddenly the subconscious assumes there is a drastic shortage of food. This scenario is in direct conflict with your primary functional need to 'stay alive at all costs.'

The brain, thinking you are in the middle of a famine, starts applying pressure in the form of pain to get you to reverse the situation. Subconsciously you are in preservation mode; it is irrelevant that you want to lose weight or indeed that it may even be beneficial for you to drop a dress size or two. Your subconscious does not rationalize; it just completes tasks. This is why 95% of people who go on a calorie-restrictive diet not only put the weight back on within five years but have on average added an additional five pounds.

So the threshold pain faded, and I was left with nothing but willpower. I started drinking again, but this time, I had a new system. Alcohol is a little creative poison and had come up with a brilliant new way for me to carry on flirting with her at a new,

103

safe level. I bought a lockable drinks cabinet and loaded it with single measure bottles of whiskey. I gave the key to my wife and explained that I was only allowed one measure a night, and if I asked for more, she was to say no. It worked well for a whole week, well worth the $350 that the cabinet cost. The plan fell down when my wife went out with friends for an evening and she took the key with her. I felt cheated because I had not even had a single drink, and she was breaking the rules; I was allowed one a day. How dare she do this to me?

I was like a petulant child. It didn't take me long to realize that the back of the cabinet was made of cheap plywood and was only tacked into place. A simple bit of leverage with a steak knife and the panel lifted up enough to squeeze a small bottle out. The new plan was dead from this point on!

Within three weeks, the pain was back and stronger than ever, and more tests eventually revealed that if I didn't want to risk liver failure within two to three years, I had to stop drinking immediately. I stopped drinking ... for three weeks, then started again. Even faced with a death sentence, I still couldn't see how giving up alcohol was a life worth living.

I can't order you to stop drinking. Your wife or husband screaming at you won't stop you. Your children begging you still won't make you see sense. Even YOU grasping the nettle and deciding to give up and resist temptation is futile. The only way you can live without this drug is to change your opinion of it fundamentally. You need to see it for what it really is: attractively packaged poison. You have probably tried to give up or cut down in the past and failed. This is because at the end of the day, you still want it, need it, and desire it. You still believe that alcohol is in some way benefiting you.

I have heard every excuse going from people just like you and just like me:

• I can't sleep without a drink before bed.

- I need it to relax.
- I am boring without a drink.
- Drinking gives me confidence.
- It helps me chill out after a hard day's work.

These are all lies, and deep down inside you know they are. If you are currently using any of these statements, from now on, see them as evidence that you are currently sitting inside a giant mousetrap resolutely believing you are perfectly safe.

The day you stop believing alcohol has any benefit and begin seeing it for what it really is, you will start to become free. As you work with me throughout this book, you will slowly begin to become aware that alcohol no longer tastes as good as it used to. You will start noticing the unpleasant taste that you have previously learned to ignore. Often people report a strange sensation of disappointment with their drink. The harshness of the poison will slowly become more and more dominant over the heaps of sugar and fruit the drinks companies use to disguise the drug hidden within. It may sound unbelievable to you at this point, but using my system, you will get to the point where you find the taste of alcoholic drinks unappealing, disappointing, and often just plain disgusting, just like you did when you first took a sneaky sip of your father's beer when you were younger.

Free Coaching Video

You don't need to hit rock bottom before you take action with this drug. The best time to have dealt with this was ten years ago. That opportunity has gone but the good news is, the next best time to take action is right now.

Watch my free video today to discover more about leveraging the power of threshold moments:

https://www.stopdrinkingexpert.com/
alcohol-and-weight-gain/

CHAPTER 8:
analysieren, zerlegen
DECONSTRUCTING
THE ADDICTION

In the interest of honesty, I will forewarn you of my intention to use a sneaky persuasion technique on you called a 'presup- *raffinierte Überzeugungstechnik* position.' Salesmen use these types of questions to appear to be offering you a choice when, in fact, all the responses serve the same purpose. A good example of a presupposition that might have been used on you, perhaps unwittingly, as a young child by your parents would be, 'Do you want to go to bed now or in ten minutes' time?' The question appears to give you the luxury of a choice, but all outcomes result in the same thing — you in bed within ten minutes.

My sneaky question to you is: do you want to stop drinking completely or just cut down a bit and repeat this course every time you lose control again until you stop? Obviously, I am try-ing to gently push you in the direction I know you should go, and despite telling you the option to cut down has repeated failure built into it, your ego still thinks it is in control and can handle anything. Be certain of this: your ego doesn't want you to stop drinking because it predicts that will result in pain/fear in the future.

I know many readers would prefer to cut down rather than stop, but the only logical solution is for you to step out of the mousetrap and never get back in. If you are dependent on alcohol and you don't want to stop, you have not quite grasped the problem. If a heroin addict came up to you and said, 'I have decided to only use drugs on a Tuesday and never any other day,' how confident are you that if you bumped into them again in a year's time that would be still the case? Alcoholism is a binary condition; it is either on or off. You can't be a little bit alcoholic in the same way you can't be a little bit pregnant!

You may need to read this book over and over before you get to this point and your decision is in harmony with my advice. Quitting completely really is the best option for you, but you must come to that decision on your own. You can't be convinced by me, your family or friends, and nobody can order you to take this stance. It has to come deep from within you. If you don't currently feel that you are still at the point where you believe you can control the situation, or that you enjoy it too much to stop completely, don't panic or beat yourself up too much. You are not alone in this struggle. In my online community, you will find people who are in the same position as you. Nobody has ever developed a drinking problem and then woken up the next morning and cured it in a eureka moment of perfection.

Part of the journey to sobriety is experiencing the futility of trying to find a way to keep the bits you like while removing the consequences you don't want. It is like trying to bail out the Titanic with a bucket; for a while, you may believe you are making headway, but very soon you start to see that you can't possibly succeed. I tried dozens and dozens of different buckets before I realized that the good parts of drinking go hand in hand with the bad, and you can't have one without the other.

Here are just a few of the buckets I thought might bail out my sinking ship:

• I will only drink on the weekends.

- I will only drink socially and never at home.
- I will drink a glass of water for every glass of alcohol I drink.
- I will take three months off the drink each year.
- I will only drink beer and no wine or spirits.
- I will only drink wine and only with food as part of a meal.

Add to that list of ridiculous theories the expensive prescription drugs I turned to. The first I tried was Disulfiram, which interferes with the way your liver processes alcohol and makes you violently ill if you drink. The problem with this drug is that it relies on your discipline to take it every morning. Alcoholics are not known for their discipline). Initially, if I knew there was a big party or social occasion I was going to, I just wouldn't take it (and so begins the failure routine. Predictably, I then loosened my rules further by only taking it Monday to Friday, allowing myself to drink at the weekends. I convinced myself that I deserved a treat at the weekends for being so good during the week.

The next stage of my defiance came when I resented the drug for preventing me from drinking during the week. I experimented with it and found that I could just about tolerate a small beer while taking it. Any more than that and the side effects would knock me flat on my back. One night I pushed it a little further and had a large beer and a glass of wine. Within 20 minutes, my head was pounding, my face blushing bright red, while my heart felt like it was trying to beat its way out of my chest cavity. For a moment, I honestly thought I might die, and the only solution was to lie in a dark room motionless for several hours until the effects subsided.

I tried other drugs, such as acamprosate calcium, which interferes with the release of dopamine, essentially taking all the pleasure out of drinking. Over time it renders your favorite tipple as pleasurable as a soft drink, and logically you only want to drink one of those when you are thirsty. Again, with this drug, the willpower or discipline required to take a daily tablet that ruins the very thing you are addicted to is a significant challenge. Add to that some pretty horrendous side effects such as dizzy spells, insomnia, dry mouth and worse, and you start to think that feeling this bad to stay off the drink is simply not worth it.

Whether it's crazy routines or pills, these methods are all simply evidence of the ego's delusion that it is in some way in control. All these methods use some form of willpower that can't possibly work because, underneath the smokescreen, you still believe that you are being deprived of what you believe to be the benefits of alcohol.

Remember, there is no such thing as failure. Things that go wrong are just events in the past, a period we are no longer concerned with. If you finish reading this book and go three weeks without a drink and then slip up, the natural temptation (and the ego's opinion) is to think that this book doesn't work, you are not strong enough, or you are always destined to be a problem drinker. Recognize this belief for what it is: the conscious mind trying to predict the future — a skill it simply doesn't have. If you fall off the wagon – big deal. Dust yourself down and carry on. When you wake in the morning, what is the point of beating yourself up about that mistake you made the night before? The past no longer exists.

Presumably, you haven't woken up with a bottle in your hand having been drinking in your sleep somehow, so right there in that moment (where all of life is lived), you are not a drinker. Equally, now that we know that the future also doesn't exist and will never exist, the fact that you had a drink the night before has no bearing on whether you will have one later that day, tomorrow, the next day, or ever again. Take each moment as it comes; every second that you decide you don't want to drink is a success.

The secret to stopping drinking is the same as the secret to getting anything else in life that you want, and this is to remain in the moment. Don't make predictions about what sort of person you will be in the future. I wouldn't ask you to predict what will happen tomorrow any more than I would ask you to perform open-heart surgery on me; you simply don't have the skills to help me. (Of course, I am recklessly playing the numbers here. One day, this book will land with an eminent heart surgeon, and he will be mortally offended by that statement.) Your journey out of the mousetrap happens by being aware of your egoic mind. Every time you find your mind wandering into the future or past, observe this happening from the point of view of an outsider. Disconnect yourself from the process; catch your ego at work.

For your conscious mind to have any power at all, it needs you to believe that you and it are the same thing. If you see it for what it is, a minor part of your mind at work, then it loses all its influence over you. Every time you catch your mind starting to worry, predict, or reflect on past events and deliberately pull yourself back into the present moment, you reduce its power over you by a fraction of one percent.

For most people, the conscious mind seizes control of them tens of thousands of times a day, and so this process isn't a magic bullet cure. I can't promise if you do this ten times, 20 times, or 50 times, you will be cured, but then you didn't become alcohol dependent overnight, and no system out there can hope to restore the correct balance in a similarly brief time period. Most other detox systems require a period of withdrawal, often called going 'cold turkey,' which for an alcoholic is at best torturous, and in worst-case scenarios can be fatal.

My method starts with your deep-seated desire to end this painful cycle and slowly deconstructs the obstacles which are preventing you from achieving your goal. Slowly, over time, as you keep resisting the attempted hijackings by your egoic mind, you will feel a sense of peace begin to build. Once you get beyond the physical dependence on alcohol, your urge to drink is generated by the wants and needs of the ego. As this diminishes, so does your desire for alcohol.

A popular question at this point is: 'How long will it take?' I can't predict the future any more than you can, so I won't even try. For most people, once they understand that everything they previously believed about alcohol having a benefit was a big fat lie and can see that a chemical imbalance is causing pain for their ego to respond to – they simply stop. For a great many people, that happens directly after reading this book. Others need a few weeks for the information to sink in, and others read the book several times before the penny drops.

Whether it takes a day or a year is irrelevant; you will find this simple process will not only remove your damaging patterns around alcohol but also all other negative habits too. Denying the ego will slowly repair everything from relationships to finances. If you want to go into greater detail about how it works then I would suggest you read my books: *Swallow The Happy Pill* and *The God Enigma*.

Once your conscious mind begins to loosen its grip on your perception of reality, this system becomes easier and easier. The secret to success is to stick at this long enough to become aware of a shift in power. So for the next 21 days, I am going to ask you to commit to doing four things every day. This does not mean after 21 days, you are no longer dependent on alcohol, or that you can stop and return to your old ways. I just know if you diligently follow the four steps I will reveal as we continue through this book, for that amount of time you will start to see something amazing happen in your life.

Free Coaching Video

Helping people rescue their lives from the grips of this nasty and devious drug is my passion. It's what I do every day of my life. I am not a doctor, but I am a man whom alcohol nearly killed, and I found a way to escape the trap before it was too late.

I would like to share my personal story with you in this video:

https://www.stopdrinkingexpert.com/mailer-craig/

CHAPTER 9: THE COST OF DRINKING

When I stopped drinking, I sat down and worked out how much I had been spending on alcohol. It's no surprise to me now that I didn't conduct this exercise while I was still drinking. I simply didn't want to acknowledge the financial cost of my habit. I didn't want to hear anything negative about alcohol. This is pure ostrich syndrome, the same technique that stopped me from going to the doctor because I was afraid he would tell me to stop drinking.

Western society acts as though alcohol is nothing more than a social pleasantry to be enjoyed with friends. In reality, it is a drug so powerful it can even prevent intelligent individuals from getting urgent medical help. Make no bones about it; this is a very dangerous and sinister drug — the ultimate wolf in sheep's clothing!

At the peak of my drinking, I was knocking back two bottles of wine a night, plus a bottle of whiskey over the weekend. At a rough guess that equates to a daily spend on alcohol of $23 per day. A weekly spend of $161 or $724 every month. Wow! No wonder I didn't want to see this figure while I was still drinking. That would have shocked and depressed me. BUT it still wouldn't have stopped me from drinking, and that is perhaps the scariest thought of all.

If I hadn't stopped drinking, it's entirely likely I would have continued consuming alcohol at that ungodly rate, or even increased it further to compensate for my growing tolerance to the effects of the drug. This means that over the next decade (if I had lived that long), I would have blown $86,940 on my addiction. Even this startling admission is only a half-truth because it doesn't allow for any of those ridiculously priced $400 bottles of 'art,' or for special occasions such as Christmas, birthdays, or any other excuse to get excessively drunk.

I was spending nearly $9,000 a year on drinking poison while telling my children and family that we couldn't afford the expensive vacations or other little luxuries that we might have been able to have if I wasn't lying to them, and of course, to myself. Hopefully, as you are starting to see, alcohol misled me. It lied to me, and it continues to lie to you. The challenge I throw down to you now is: What are you going to do about it?

I encourage you to honestly do this exercise for yourself and calculate how much money you are spending on common drug addiction. You will no doubt come up with an amount that you could spend on a hundred different and better things. Sadly, the financial cost is almost insignificant when compared to everything else alcohol has stolen from you.

Alcohol affects everyone differently, but for me, it made me sleepy. In a practical sense, what this meant was when I got home from work at, let's say, 6.00 pm. The first glass of wine was poured by 6.05 pm. Less than an hour later, the first bottle was gone. By 8.00 pm I had moved on to and consumed about two-thirds of the second bottle of wine (I would never drink the full second bottle because then I could claim I had not drunk two full bottles of wine if anyone asked). At this point in the evening, after nearly two bottles of wine, I could hardly keep my eyes open. I would spend the next thirty minutes staring at the clock wishing it was later so I could go to bed at a decent time. It would be rare for me to make it to 9.00 pm, normally collapsing unconscious into bed between 8.30 pm and 8.45 pm.

I would sleep poorly, waking several times to use the toilet and a few more times gasping for water to deal with the dehydration. My bloodshot eyes would blink open at 6.00 am, and I would head to work exhausted.

This was my life for longer than I care to admit, and while alcohol may not have the same outcome for you, there will almost certainly be another negative side effect to replace it. In my case, let's say a more reasonable bedtime for a nine-to-five office worker is around 11.00 pm. This means that my drinking took me offline for an additional 17 hours per week. Over ten years, I spent 9,100 hours knocked out and unconscious because of my drug addiction. That is time I will never get back. How many opportunities and experiences can you fit into nearly 10,000 hours?

The mind boggles.

The situation is even bleaker because I am a father; it's not just my time I was throwing away. Allow me to expand on this point to ram home the gloomy message of what my drinking did.

If you are a parent, I apologize for what I am about to ask you to do next. If you are a visual or kinesthetic character type, then this may be traumatic and painful for you to imagine, but please bear with me because I am doing this not to be cruel or give you nightmares, but to make a valuable point. Imagine that tomorrow your child is abducted, and you never see them again. Immediately, such a horrific suggestion may remind you of what happened to the McCann family while on vacation in sunny Portugal a few years ago.

On Thursday, 3rd May 2007, Jerry and Kate McCann put their little daughter Madeline to bed for the last time. At some point before midnight, she was taken from her bed and has never been seen since.

If that happened to you and there was absolutely nothing you could do to prevent it happening, let me ask you, what price would you put on an hour spent with your daughter? If a few months later it were possible to buy the opportunity to see your child again and spend just one hour with them, what would you be prepared to pay?

Is it $1,000, $10,000, $100,000, or is it priceless? Would you pay everything you had just to spend that one hour with your child? I know for me the answer is the latter, and yet alcohol (the social drug) made me throw away over 9,000 hours that I could have spent with my lovely children, Jordan and Aoife.

My children are the most precious things in my life, and yet a drug that people insist is just a bit of harmless fun, a beverage that they say is vital to the success of a party, a drink they demand must be consumed or you will be labeled boring and weird, somehow this 'innocent' substance made me willingly give away 758 priceless days with my children.

I am going to take a break from writing at this point because I am so angry and feel so cheated that I don't think I can continue.

I will close this chapter by giving you one question to think about. What has alcohol stolen from you?

Is it your health, your time, your promotion, your money, your wife, your husband, your career? It may be one thing, or it might be many, but as sure as night follows day, make no mistake about it, you are the victim of serious theft. Unless you wake up and realize that the bottle of alcohol you thought was your friend is your worst enemy, then you will be a victim tomorrow, the day after, and every day until the truth dawns on you.

The average drinker who joins my online stop drinking club is spending around $3,000 a year on alcohol! That might sound a lot, and the tendency of any drinker is to assume they are nowhere near that amount. But $3,000 is less than ten bucks a day, and so if you are one of those people who drink a bottle of wine a day plus a bit more at the weekend, then you are way over that figure. Let's keep the glass half full (excuse the pun), and we will stick with the average. Every person I have ever spoken to has agreed that they could find something important to do with $3,000.

If I gave you that money today and told you to spend it however you like, what would you do with it? Maybe:

- Take the kids to Disneyland?
- Put it towards a new car?
- Take a romantic vacation?
- Put it towards the college fund?
- Pay a medical bill or for a procedure?
- Pay off a credit card?

Whether you would use it to make life bearable or to simply add pleasure for you and those you love, that money is there and waiting for you to do any one of those things. You don't have to ask your boss for a raise, work overtime, or change job – it is already yours! To get it, all you have to do is step outside your current situation and see that alcohol is not your friend, helping you deal with a difficult life, but rather your enemy, deliberately stealing all those wonderful things from you and your family.

My challenge to you is to put this book down and do the exercise that 95% of drinkers refuse even to consider. Sit down and _ca. 3.500 €!_ honestly work out how much you spend on alcohol in a year. Make sure you include those lunchtime drinks with clients, weekend binges, and special occasions such as Christmas and birthdays, those times when you treat yourself to much more expensive poison than usual. Come up with your golden number and then think about what you would do with that money if somebody gave it to you in a lump sum today.

Next, imagine what you would rather spend it on, whether it is taking the trip to Florida you have always wanted or clearing

Caro's Miete

the debt that just won't leave you alone. Get on the Internet and find an image that represents what you want. Print it out and stick it on the bathroom mirror or refrigerator, somewhere where you will see it every day. If you ever take that image down without having completed the goal, you will know that alcohol still has a hold over you.

Free Coaching Video

This is a powerful moment of change in your life. You are finally dealing with the thing that you thought was your friend but actually turned out to be your worst enemy.

Let me ask you a BIG question, what will happen if you don't deal with this? Watch my video for answers.

https://www.stopdrinkingexpert.com/dont-quit-drinking/

CHAPTER 10
SUPPLEMENTING
THE IMBALANCE

Warning: Do not take any supplements listed here without consulting your doctor or other healthcare professional. If your current dependency causes you to experience traumatic physical symptoms such as spasms, fitting, fever, or vomiting when you stop, you will need to see your doctor. They will be able to give you prescription medication to help suppress these unpleasant and potentially dangerous side effects while you go through the kick.

I am assuming you came to this book with a desire to stop drinking but were not quite sure how to go about it. I am hoping that by now your desire has intensified. You now see alcohol for what it really is, and you are determined never to drink that foul-tasting, life-destroying poison that is alcohol again. If you are still hoping to go back to drinking one day, or are planning just to cut down, let me explain why that is a terrible idea.

All addictive drugs have what is known as a kick, the period after you stop taking them in which the side effects occur. Luckily for you, we are talking about an alcohol kick, which is relatively mild compared to other street drugs. The reason heroin is so difficult to quit is that the kick is so intense and painful that the user has to endure agony knowing that all the pain could vanish in a split second by just taking another hit of the drug.

Alcohol withdrawal begins from the moment you take your last sip and will reach its peak intensity between 24 and 48 hours later. This is why many people become evening drinkers and the first thing they do when they get home after a hard day at work is reach for the bottle opener. As they arrive home, they are exactly mid-way through the most powerful phase of the withdrawal process. Alcohol withdrawal is so subtle that we are unable to identify the symptoms unless we are aware of what to look for. Withdrawal from alcohol feels like a general feeling of unease. To the everyday person, it may feel a little like stress or anxiety. This is why people incorrectly claim that a drink when they get home from work helps them unwind. The only thing that first drink does is to turn off the withdrawal symptoms of the previous day's drinking. So to a certain extent, it's true: they do feel instantly less stressed because the general unease and anxiety directly created by the alcohol has now gone, but, if they hadn't drunk the day before, it wouldn't have been there in the first place. So all they are fixing is the previous day's mistake.

The full chemical withdrawal from alcohol, regardless of the amount you drink, lasts around two weeks, climbing to a climax around 36 hours after the last drink and slowly fading away to near zero after a couple of weeks. Because of the hard wiring you have constructed in your brain, and your overactive hypothalamus, you may never achieve total zero, but every day you don't drink, the base state of withdrawal drops a little further.

This extended withdrawal period is precisely why you cannot safely have 'just one drink.' That first drink is the reason why 95% of people trying to quit with willpower fail. One sip of alcohol may take less than five seconds to consume but will start an unstoppable process that will last at least two weeks. During that period, a new chemical imbalance will force you to crave another drink.

There are only two ways to relieve the discomfort and pain of the craving. The first is to take a drink of alcohol. Yes, you will get short-term relief as the alcohol causes the flooding of the chemicals you crave. Then as the alcohol begins to leave your body you will experience the discomfort and pain again, prompting you to drink again to get relief, and so you get caught in a never-ending loop. The second is to not take the drink and give the body enough time to rid itself of the alcohol, which it will if you give it long enough. Only one of these solutions doesn't create another problem the next day, and I don't need to tell you which one.

If for the briefest moment you start to think, 'Just one drink won't do any harm,' or, 'I will only have one glass of wine with my evening meal,' you are willingly stepping back into the mousetrap and assuming that this time you are safe; one more poke at the cheese won't make any difference!

If you have been consuming an unhealthy amount of alcohol (not that there is a healthy amount) for a significant period, your brain and body will have already adapted to the new (unhealthy) reality you have created. It's this power of human adaptability that is often underestimated and provides a convenient smokescreen to the problem that lies hidden beneath. If people dropped down dead after a week of heavy drinking, do you think the current worldwide epidemic of alcoholism would exist?

There is a famous story of an elderly man who had given a pint of blood once a month for nearly forty years of his life. Eventually, the time came where the blood bank advised him that his blood was no longer suitable for donation and while they were very grateful for his years of generosity they could no longer use his blood for medical purposes. The gentleman stopped making his monthly trip to the donation center, and it wasn't long before he started to feel very ill. He repeatedly visited his doctor complaining of vague symptoms of unease and discomfort. It took quite some time before they were able to establish that his problem was that he had too much blood in his system. His body had adapted to losing at least a pint of blood every month without fail. He had become conditioned to producing blood at a rate to compensate, and it is only when the situation changed that the adaptation became noticeable.

You have adapted to poison being present in your system, and when you stop drinking, you may become aware of this adaptation for the first time. This feeling of unease is not caused by the loss of alcohol, but rather it is a clear indication of what your body has had to do to keep you alive in such a polluted lifestyle. When you quit the alcohol, your brain chemistry will once again be out of balance for a while until it readapts to life as it is supposed to be lived. Our goal is to take the struggle and pain out of giving up drinking, so it's important that you take some supplements to ensure you don't have to deal with a low mental state during the kick period.

So here is how you break the loop once and for all. **First, stop drinking, I mean today. Right now.** Unlike before when you have had this brave moment, we are going to do something vitally different. We are going to stop the first imbalance from triggering the second imbalance. Remember, for the next two weeks you may feel uneasy, uncomfortable, and anxious. This is caused by the kick from alcohol, an addictive drug. The good news is once you've been sober for about two weeks, the symptoms are so mild you can't distinguish them from the genuine emotions of daily life. (Again, If your current dependency causes you to experience traumatic physical symptoms such as spasms, fitting, fever, or vomiting when you stop, you will need to see your doctor. They will be able to give you prescription medication to help suppress these unpleasant side effects while you go through the kick.)

This time when you quit, we are not going to leave you at the mercy of your imbalanced brain chemistry. So the second thing you we are going to do is incorporate supplements to help get you through the kick. Balanced nutrition is important for everyone, whether they are problem drinkers or not. The following are recommendations that could be helpful for the general population as most of us don't get the vital nutrients we need from our depleted diet, alone. However, as heavy drinkers they are especially important to get through the kick. We are starting with a handicap and need to repair damage done from years of drinking.

It's important that you follow these recommendations to the letter. I understand there is a cost involved with buying high-quality supplements, but I promise it will be significantly less than you are currently spending on alcohol. Do not be tempted to omit any of the recommended supplements as they are all important and work well together to achieve our desired outcome of repairing the damage done and maintain permanent sobriety. Again, check with your doctor before adding supplements, especially if you have an underlying medical condition or are taking any medications.

SUPPLEMENT SHOPPING LIST:

Omega 3

We know that essential fats in the brain are vital for proper brain function, and by that, I mean having correctly functioning neurotransmitters and receptors. If you have ever spilled oil or grease on a piece of fabric, you will know that water won't even touch it. To get rid of an oil stain, you need to add a chemical solvent to break it down. You won't be surprised to hear that one solvent that is particularly good at this job is alcohol. While this is good news if you need to rescue an expensive sofa with a nasty oil stain, it is very bad news for us problem drinkers. Alcohol destroys essential fats; it rips through like napalm.

As a heavy drinker, you almost certainly have an essential fat deficiency, which means your neurotransmitters and receptors cannot function correctly, and your body struggles to maintain dopamine and serotonin at sufficient levels to make you feel good.

The two specific essential fats that we need when we stop drinking are Eicosapentaenoic acid (EHA) and Docosahexaenoic acid (DHA). You can find both of these in a high-quality Omega 3 supplement. Do not buy cod liver oil tablets as they contain a large amount of vitamin A, which may combine with some of the other supplements I am going to recommend and may cause some rather unpleasant side effects.

Multivitamin

The multivitamin is like a broadsword covering most of your needs up to somewhere near the Recommended Daily Allowance (RDA) amount. However, as problem drinkers, we are not your average human beings; we need some of the vitamins and minerals in significantly higher dosages than the standard individual. The multivitamin you choose must contain the following:

Vitamin C

Virtually all High Street multivitamins will contain vitamin C (ascorbic acid), but only the comprehensive A to Z brands will provide the full range of elements. Additionally, I advise you to further increase your intake by eating significantly more citrus fruits, or by adding another vitamin C supplement.

Magnesium

Magnesium is an essential mineral for staying healthy and is required for more than 300 biochemical reactions in the body. Multiple health benefits of magnesium include transmission of nerve impulses, body temperature regulation, detoxification, energy production, and the formation of healthy bones and teeth. Because there may not be enough magnesium in your multivitamin, and because it is important to take with your vitamin D supplement, I recommend purchasing an additional magnesium supplement. (See further discussion of magnesium below.)

Zinc

Zinc is an essential mineral that is naturally present in some foods, added to others, and available as a dietary supplement. Zinc plays a role in immune function, protein synthesis, wound healing, DNA synthesis, and cell division. Zinc also supports normal growth and development during pregnancy, childhood, and adolescence and is required for proper sense of taste and smell . A daily intake of zinc is required to maintain a steady state because the body has no specialized zinc storage system.

Vitamin B Complex

Many individuals are deficient in B12, such as smokers, pregnant and breast-feeding women, strict vegetarians, the elderly, and — no surprise here — heavy drinkers. Alcohol decreases your body's ability to absorb vitamin B12 and flushes it from your system. Vitamin B12 can be found in most multivitamins, but not in the amount that you will need as a heavy drinker, so I recommend adding an additional vitamin B12 supplement.

Vitamin B12 is a water-soluble vitamin that is naturally present in some foods, added to others, and available as a dietary supplement and a prescription medication. Vitamin B12 is responsible for the smooth functioning of several critical body processes. It is required for proper red blood cell formation, neurological function, and DNA synthesis. A deficiency can result in a host of illnesses such as anemia, constipation, soreness of the mouth, asthma, vision problems, poor memory, and a low sperm count.

Other symptoms of deficiency can be hard to distinguish from depression, such as fatigue, weakness, loss of appetite, and weight loss. So, we are especially interested in vitamin B12's ability to boost levels of serotonin, melatonin, and dopamine, the "feel good" neurochemicals.

Health benefits of vitamin B12 may include:

- A decrease in fatigue and lethargy. B12 is needed to convert carbohydrates into glucose in the body, thus leading to energy production and a decrease in fatigue and lethargy in the body.
- Healthy regulation of the nervous system, reducing depression, stress, and brain shrinkage.
- Healthy digestive system.
- Protection against heart disease, stroke, and high blood pressure by curbing and improving unhealthy cholesterol levels.
- Healthy skin, hair, and nails. B12 helps in cell reproduction and renewal.
- Increased protection against some cancers, including breast, colon, lung, and prostate cancer.

Vitamin D

Vitamin D can be found in your multi-vitamin, but not in nearly the amount you need, so I recommend adding an additional vitamin D supplement.

Vitamin D is a fat-soluble vitamin is important for healthy functioning of many body processes. It is hugely important for its role in promoting calcium absorption in the gut and supporting bone growth. A deficiency in vitamin D has been linked to diseases including dementia, Crohn's Disease, cancer and the repeated appearance of the common cold and flu.

There is a pandemic of vitamin D deficiency that is causing ill health, lethargy, and weight gain around the world. The problem has been created by our modern lifestyle choices (not the least of which is increased alcohol consumption), several key incorrect assumptions, and the cutthroat dollars and cents mentality behind our medical research techniques.

I have witnessed the effects of Vitamin D deficiency first-hand. A few years ago, my daughter Aoife started to complain about pain in her bones and skin. She also started to get random and volatile mood swings and erratic behavior. As she was just entering that difficult phase of life that involves leaving childhood behind and becoming a teenager, we initially attributed these symptoms to growing pains and the general teenage moodiness all kids go through.

However, the symptoms slowly got worse until she was taking an unhealthy amount of pain relievers just to get through each day. The doctors initially assumed an autoimmune disorder was most likely, as her mother had already been diagnosed with Lupus (SLE). Thankfully, the blood test was negative for the SLE markers and any other serious conditions.

Coincidently this was around the time I was starting to research vitamin D and magnesium, and it struck me that a lot of the symptoms I was reading about sounded very similar to Aoife's symptoms. I suggested to the doctor that we test for these. While the results showed that Aoife's magnesium levels were fine, they also showed that she was severely deficient in vitamin D and they were going to prescribe a daily supplement.

Health benefits of vitamin D may include:

- Promotion of healthy bones and teeth.
- Support for immune, brain, and nervous system health.
- Regulation of insulin levels, supporting diabetes man-

agement.
- Support for lung function and cardiovascular health.

There are a few false assumptions about vitamin D:

False Assumption One

We can get all the vitamin D we need from a few minutes of sunshine each day.

As most people know, exposure to UV rays from sunshine is a necessary step in activating the vitamin D that is absorbed from your diet. The problem is, over the last century our lifestyles have changed faster and more profoundly than in any period before. Human beings in the past have been predominately outdoor, manual workers until relatively recently. Agricultural and industrial work dominated until the information age came along. We no longer work the fields but rather tend to sit in front of a computer monitor all day long before going home to then sit in front of a bigger screen until bedtime. Children no longer play games on the streets and climb trees for fun. You are much more likely to see them sitting in front of a games console killing zombies with an AK47 (unaware of the irony that they look a bit like zombies themselves).

In addition, that assumption is too generic. Sun exposure might be perfectly adequate when applied to fair-skinned people living near the equator. But what about everyone else? The darker your skin, the less vitamin D you create, and the strength of the UV rays from the sun dramatically decreases when you live far from the equator.

Finally, we have become so terrified of the sun that we now routinely apply sunscreen to ourselves and our children as part of our daily routine. A sunscreen with a high sun protection factor will block many of the UV rays needed by your skin to produce vitamin D.

The reality is that our lifestyles have slowly changed and moved us out of the sunlight. It will be several hundred thousand years before evolution catches up. So you can either wait or start taking a supplement – your choice!

False Assumption Two

Vitamin D is just another vitamin and no more important than any of the others.

Our blasé approach to supplements causes a problem here because it fails to give vitamin D the spotlight it deserves. The problem has more to do with how we talk about it, as it is actually an essential hormone, not a vitamin, at all.

A hormone is a substance that is produced in one part of the body but has a wide-ranging effect on various other important parts of the body, such as the brain, heart, and other vital organs.

Vitamin D is as essential to good health as sleep, food, and exercise.

False Assumption Three:

If vitamin D is so important, surely my doctor would test for vitamin deficiency and recommend it.

The reality is that you are most likely to have never been tested for vitamin D deficiency, and here is the reason why:

Vitamin D fails to make it onto the medical training agenda and into doctors' surgeries (a.k.a. clinics or practices) due to the dollars and cents mentality of our medical research.

Pharmaceutical companies searching for a cure for cancer aren't doing so out of the goodness of their hearts. Discovering a cure and having a monopoly on the treatment means one thing: massive profits.

Vitamin D is inexpensive and freely available around the world, over the counter and without prescription, and therefore, it is of no value to the medical research companies out to invent the next miracle cure. Sadly, most of the training received by doctors is still heavily influenced by major pharmaceutical companies.

With the limited information being given to the medical community and out of date dosage recommendations, you have vitamin D left sitting on the shelf.

<u>Vitamin D and Weight Loss</u>

Before we leave the subject of vitamin D, I should say something about vitamin D and weight loss. In addition to all the other health benefits of vitamin D, there is an interesting side effect of weight reduction (or perhaps a better phrase would be weight correction). I am not suggesting taking a D supplement for this reason alone, but it is a pleasant added bonus to what I consider to be a true miracle addition to any diet.

There are a lot of empty calories in alcohol, and I am sure my unhealthy consumption of a daily bottle of wine added to the extra 60 pounds of fat I was carrying around. So, for many people hooked on alcohol and wanting to stop, they can add potential weight loss as a bonus benefit.

There have been several studies that have linked vitamin D to weight loss. Vitamin D has been shown to be very effective in increasing the amount of body fat loss while increasing energy levels. By increasing your energy levels, your body can overcome chronic fatigue and lethargic moods.

So how much do you take?

Again, I will remind you that I am not a doctor, and you must do your own research before taking any of the supplements. All I can do here is to tell you what I personally take and explain why I do so.

The 'out of date' RDA for vitamin D that you will likely see quoted on the side of your multivitamin bottle is 200 IU per day. When I discovered what the leading experts in this field are now recommending, I was blown away by just how inaccurate the government official RDA is.

Vitamin D can be taken monthly, weekly, or daily. Personally, I take it as part of my morning routine. That way, I can keep a close eye on what I am doing and how it is affecting me. I recommend adding a vitamin D supplement to your diet at an amount of 20 IU per pound of body weight. For example, I weigh in at 192 lbs, and so I take 3900 IU per day. You can expect to see noticeable improvements with health, mobility, and weight between two weeks and three months after starting supplementation.

Obviously, you will need to recalculate your dosage on a regular basis as your body weight starts to fall.

If you are interested in reading more about the Vitamin D pandemic and why this hormone is so vital and yet so overlooked I recommend reading *The Vitamin D Cure* by James Dowd and *The Power of Vitamin D* by Sarfraz Zaidi.

Vitamin K2

There is a delicate balance between Vitamin D and K2. It is vital if you are supplementing your diet with high strength Vitamin D that you also take a daily Vitamin K2 tablet.

Magnesium

You will find magnesium in your multi-vitamin, but like vitamin K2 it goes hand-in-hand with your vitamin D supplement and I recommend adding an additional magnesium supplement.

Magnesium is a nutrient that the body needs to stay healthy. Magnesium is important for many processes in the body, including regulating muscle and nerve function, blood sugar levels, and blood pressure and making protein, bone, and DNA.

Good dietary sources of magnesium include nuts (especially almonds), whole grains, wheat germ, fish, and green leafy vegetables. As with most nutrients, daily needs for magnesium cannot be met from food alone, which is why dietary magnesium supplements are recommended as well.

Health benefits of magnesium may include:

- Prevention and reversal of osteoporosis
- Reduced risk of stroke and cardiovascular disease
- Regulation of blood pressure
- Decreased risk of diabetes by controlling blood glu-

cose levels
- Relief from panic attacks, stress, and anxiety
- Relief from symptoms of menopause and premen-strual syndrome (PMS)
- Reduced risk of premature labor

5-HTP

Another important piece of the supplement jigsaw puzzle is related to the amino acid tryptophan, which is needed to create serotonin, one of the key neurotransmitters involved in maintaining a positive emotional state. Serotonin deficiency is a common feature of depression. As a problem drinker, you are highly likely to be low on this vital chemical. Supporting a healthy serotonin level is a crucial component of my stop drinking method.

Tryptophan is found in turkey, soybeans, tuna, halibut and other fish. The easiest way to get an adequate amount of tryptophan is to take a supplement called 5-HTP, which stands for 5-Hydroxytryptophan.

Not everyone should take this supplement. Though side effects of 5-HTP are typically mild and may include nausea, heartburn, gas, and feelings of fullness, taking a higher than recommended dose could result in serotonin syndrome, a dangerous condition caused by too much serotonin in the body. **Because of the potential for side effects and interactions with medications, you should consult with your healthcare provider before taking 5-HTP or other supplements.**

Those who should *not* take 5-HTP include:

- People taking anti-depressants.
- People with liver disease.
- Pregnant women.
- Women who are breastfeeding.

Those who should talk to their healthcare provider before taking 5-HTP are:

- People with high blood pressure.
- People with diabetes.
- People using one of the following medications:

Carbidopa

Tramadol (Ultram)

Dextromethorphan (Robitussin DM, and others)

Meperidine (Demerol)

Triptans (used to treat migraines)

- Naratriptan (Amerge)
- Rizatriptan (Maxalt)
- Sumatriptan (Imitrex)
- Zolmitriptan (Zomig)

If after having read the precautions and talked to your doctor, you are cleared to take 5-HTP, here is what I recommend:

Take two 50mg capsules about 30 minutes before bed with a small sugary drink. This could be a mug of hot chocolate or even just a piece of chocolate if you prefer.

The reason for this specific 5-HTP ritual is that this amino acid is transported to the brain by insulin, which is created by the pancreas as a reaction to consuming sugar. If there is plenty of insulin rushing around your system, the 5-HTP will reach its target more quickly and more effectively. (If you have diabetes, you should skip this step.) We take this supplement last thing at night because the brain converts serotonin into melatonin, which calms our mind and prepares us for the sleep cycle. So, a pleasant side effect of more serotonin is better sleep. After a relatively short period, you should notice that you find it easier to get to sleep and feel more rested when you awake in the morning.

Curcumin

We all know that alcohol is terrible for the health and wellbeing of our liver. No matter what is the the root cause of liver injury, the medical dangers are significant, pushing individuals to search for techniques to sustain regular operation and safeguard against the advancement of cirrhosis. Sadly, depending upon the cause of liver harm, therapy choices are restricted, which has resulted in a rise in study interest in the field. Presently, one distinct target of study interest is alcohol dehydrogenase, a chemical located mainly in the liver organ.

Alcohol dehydrogenase is responsible for mobilizing the oxidation and elimination of different alcohols and aldehydes (which are natural particles identical to alcohols, but with a somewhat different molecular framework). That makes alcohol dehydrogenase a major player in some of the purifying processes that shield the liver from harm. More specifically, when elevated amounts of poisons like alcohol, 'unhealthy' nutritional fats, and specific medicines reach the liver, they can bring about the creation of free radicals that escalate irritation and specifically harm hepatic cells — the functions of alcohol dehydrogenase help to combat these consequences and reduce the harm.

Developing research suggests that curcumin, the active substance in turmeric extract, may successfully assist the function of alcohol dehydrogenase in a manner that shields the liver against harm. Even though medical trials have yet to be carried out, there are numerous initial reports in rodents that provide crucial insight into the systems through which natural curcumin supplementation may offer defensive perks for individuals.

The initial indication that there may be a connection between alcohol dehydrogenase and curcumin came in 2011 when a team of Eastern analysts released a post illustrating their discovery of the curcumin metabolic process in a digestive bacterium. Intriguingly, the distinct curcumin-metabolizing chemical they discovered (which they called NADPH-dependent curcumin/dihydro curcumin reductase or CurA), bore a considerable pattern resemblance to widely known molecules in the alcohol dehydrogenase family. This data offered an initial idea that it might be feasible for curcumin to communicate directly with the alcohol dehydrogenase molecules in the human liver.

The greatest proof for an explicit connection between curcumin and alcohol dehydrogenase, however, came in 2013, when a team of scientists from a number of colleges in South Korea worked together on an attempt to explore the defense that modest amounts of curcumin might deliver against liver harm brought on by persistent alcohol consumption and a high-fat diet. So as to look into this issue, they treated rodent models on high-alcohol, high-fat eating plans with a couple of different dosages of curcumin (0.02% and 0.05% body weight) for six weeks. At both amounts, they observed considerable benefits. Along with decreasing the function of molecules that are understood to result in liver damage, the curcumin supplements stopped the alcohol-induced inhibition of alcohol dehydrogenase function to a statistically notable level. Notably, curcumin supplements also resulted in considerable decreases in plasma levels of leptin, free fatty acids, and triglyceride levels, all of which bring about swelling and liver harm. These results function as initial proof that by tweaking key molecules like alcohol dehydrogenase, curcumin supplements can successfully protect against liver damage.

The results of the 2013 investigation were later sustained by a report out of George Washington University, in which the analysts again disclosed a link between supplementary curcumin intake and liver injury in rodents. Like the Korean analysts, the investigation unit from George Washington set out to look into this link by treating rodents on high-fat, high-alcohol meal plans with curcumin, this time around with supplements of 150 mg/kg/day, every day for eight weeks. By the end of the treatment duration, they discovered that the rodents in the therapy cluster were shielded from ethanol-induced hepatic steatosis (that is, the build-up of fat in the liver) and presented reduced amounts of oxidative stress and liver trauma markers (as determined in blood samples) than those that did not take the supplements. Therefore, like past scientists, they reasoned that curcumin supplements might offer safeguards from liver harm.

For former problem drinkers who are looking for to prevent the health risks of liver damage-- whether it is connected with alcohol usage, dietary fats, prescription medications, or inflammatory bowel disorders-- a curcumin supplement might offer restorative advantages. Future medical analysis will probably shed more light on the impacts in human beings. However, for now, the animal's investigations indicate that it might be worth looking into curcumin supplements as an option and tracking their influences on the individual client's liver.

Excited? I was and that's why I still have it in my supplementation routine today. It is crucial to pick a curcumin supplement with high bioavailability. Although the scientists from Korea revealed that the rodents in the report were treated with 'low-dose' curcumin supplements, curcumin is widely known for its low bioavailability, indicating that it is inadequately absorbed in the GI region. This means its effect on the body may be reduced by formulation, even when it is consumed at greater amounts. To optimize the probability that a curcumin supplement will be absorbed, metabolized, and supply the preferred defensive advantages, individuals and specialists should, consequently, try to find curcumin supplements that were especially created for optimum bioavailability.

Supplements Shopping List

- ✓ Omega 3 capsules (1000 mg)
- ✓ Broad spectrum multivitamin
- ✓ B Vitamin complex
- ✓ Vitamin D (20iu per day / per lb of body weight)
- ✓ Vitamin K2
- ✓ Magnesium
- ✓ Curcumin BCM95 capsules (500mg)

Free Coaching Video

Find out more about supplements to make quitting drinking easy in today's free video and blog post:

https://www.stopdrinkingexpert.com/
supplements-to-stop-drinking/

CHAPTER 11:
CONTROLLING THE
EVIL CLOWN

It will appear to the casual reader that you are now into what could be described as 'the cure' section of the book. In these shorter chapters, I am giving you specific things to do that I know will help you stop drinking. However, if you have skipped forward to this point, you will miss the whole point of the book. My method is a six-step program, and the 'cure' is delivered through every chapter and not just the final four.

At this point, I don't want you to be worried that up to now I appear to have only given you a list of vitamins to buy from the health food store. You may worry that it sounds too easy and are perhaps thinking surely there must be more to it than popping a few pills.

Don't worry, because there is, and indeed, after reading this book if the only thing you did was to go out and buy the supplements I mentioned in Chapter 10, I am almost certain you would not stop drinking as a result.

If you only follow through on half the steps in this book, then there is only a very slim chance you will give up the alcohol. So finely balanced is the process that even if you complete five of the six steps, I still won't express my total confidence in you to achieve the sober outcome you desire. This method works for so many people because the whole is far greater than the sum of its parts. It's the combination of multiple levels of a theory that combine to cause a paradigm shift significant enough to change your thinking and subconscious programming.

Whether you believe in a step or not, please do not remove it from the method. Each one of the six steps works hand in hand with the next to create the desired outcome.

The first step you achieved long before you even picked this book up — you made the decision that you are sick and tired of feeling sick and tired. You developed an awareness that alcohol is starting to create more problems than it solves. This is a beautiful stage to get to because at this point you stop being a part of the 80% who refuse to admit that they have a problem and you move into an elite bunch of people who are ready to take action.

Step two was what I explained to you over the first nine chapters of this book. To completely claim step two has been completed, you should by this point agree with me that alcohol is not an inoffensive social pleasantry, but a deviously packaged and promoted addictive drug.

You should now clearly see the lies you previously believed for what they are and cannot logically see any benefit to the further consumption of alcohol. If this is not the case and you still believe that if you stop drinking, you will deny yourself something special, then this method and any other method you care to try will fail.

It is virtually impossible to give up something that you still believe has a benefit in your life. This is exactly why 95% of alcoholics who join AA end up relapsing. If you still want to drink because you believe it tastes good, makes you more confident, helps you relax, or any of the other lies, then do yourself a favor:

• Turn back to page one and start again. Many need to read this book numerous times before the penny drops.

· Start researching the true effects of alcohol for yourself and get piles of evidence to demonstrate the reality of this drug.

· Take a look at my other books on the subject, including *The Alcohol Illusion*, which explains how deceptive alcohol can be.

Unless you can honestly say that you feel differently about alcohol now, there is no point buying the vitamins and supplements mentioned in step three. There is no advantage in moving onto step four if the first and second parts of the method are not 100% nailed on.

If you are still reading, congratulations! That means you have checked off step one and two and now have a list in your hand ready to take to the health food store that says:

1. Broad-spectrum 'once a day' multivitamin
2. B Vitamin Complex
3. Omega 3 1000MG capsules
4. Magnesium tablets
5. Vitamin C tablets.
6. Vitamin D tablets 2500 IU
7. BCM-95 tablets

*If you are taking any other prescription medication, please check with your doctor before taking 5-HTP.

You are now ready for step four. This section addresses one of the most important keys to stopping drinking – the egoic tendency to predict failure.

I need you to become aware of your conscious mind's attempts to seize control. It happens so often that this step can appear to be quite a challenge. Sometimes it appears so monumental a task that you are not quite sure where to start.

Let me give you a list of examples of your ego attempting a hijack you:

• You try a dress on and it feels a bit tight. You start to feel bad about yourself because it used to fit perfectly. This is your ego pulling the past into the future.

• Your boss criticizes your work, and you start to think about all the things that he gets wrong. How dare he talk to you like that? Does he not know how much time you spent on that project, etc.? This is an attack on your ego, and your ego is responding.

• You are driving, and someone cuts you off and beeps their horn at you, and instantly you beep back, outraged that they are blaming you for their mistake! You consider for a brief moment what you should do next. This is an attack on your ego, and your ego is responding.

• You are going to a party later, and you find yourself worrying about how you will cope without a drink. This is your ego predicting failure.

All thoughts of the past and future must be generated by the ego/conscious because from the subconscious mind's point of view, they don't exist and so can't be considered. These thoughts are not universally negative, but they are highly unlikely to be positive. For example, even if you get excited thinking about seeing your children or partner later, there is always a negative connotation attached to the anticipation. For example, you are thinking, 'I can't wait to get home and play with my children. I wish it were 5.00 pm already.'

Even though you might consider this to be a positive thought process, the ego is still suggesting that happiness lies in a different time and not in the precise moment you are currently experiencing.

You don't need to use willpower to try to stop this from happening; all I am asking you to do is be aware of it. Laugh at it when you spot it, welcome it back like an old friend. It is actu-

143

tatsächlich

ally your awareness of it happening that causes it to lose power. Once you start realizing that your ego and you are not one and the same, amazing and beautiful things start to appear in your life.

I am acutely aware it may sound far too simple and perhaps even too good to be true. But even that is just a conscious prediction of failure generated by your ego.

nimm einen Vertrauensvorschuss an

Don't take my word for it, take a leap of faith and for the next 21 days assume its true... just watch the difference!

The egoic need to predict the future is a particular problem for someone trying to quit drinking alcohol because it is a powerful motivator of human behavior and will provide quite compelling arguments that your life will be less enjoyable without alcohol. The ego hates any form of change that comes from an external force; it simply doesn't like anything that implies that it is not in full control of your life.

Here are some of the common false predictions generated by the ego in response to stopping drinking:

- Going to social occasions will no longer be any fun.
- Vacations will be less pleasurable in the sober future.
- You will have no way of relaxing after a stressful day.
- There will be no way to celebrate in the future.
- You will struggle to get to sleep.

If any of those thoughts have entered your mind as you consider taking the next step on your journey to a dry life, I would like you to recognize that they are nothing but the senile ramblings of your ego attempting to do something it is completely incapable of doing — predicting the future. When you catch yourself thinking about drinking, consider whether any part of the thought is coming from a memory of the past or a prediction of the future and recognize at this point that it is only the ego in a panic about what you are doing. Pull yourself back into the moment that we call the 'now.'

Henrik Edburg puts it well when he says there are lots of advantages to living in the moment, including:

- Clarity. When you are in the moment, you have a much better focus, and things flow naturally out of you. This is very useful in conversations, at work, while writing, or even while doing fun stuff such as playing golf.

- Calmness. You feel centered, relaxed, and whatever you do, you do more easily. Since you are not projecting into a possible future or reflecting on previous experiences, there is very little fear holding you back.

- Positivity. Since there is little fear, there are few negative emotions when you are in the present. Instead, you move around the positive part of the emotional scale.

How do you actually return to the present moment?

There are seven ways. But before we get to them, I'd just like to add that this is a skill. You will slip back into involuntarily thinking about the future/past. But the more time and effort you spend connecting with the moment, the easier it gets reconnecting with it and staying there longer.

1. Focus on what's right in front of you — or around you — or on you. Use your senses. Just look at what's right in front of you right now. Listen to the sounds around you. Feel the fabric of your clothes and focus on how they feel.

2. Focus on your breathing.
Take a couple of dozen belly breaths and focus your mind on your inhalations and exhalations. This will align you with the present moment once again.

3. Focus on your inner body.
This is a bit similar to focusing on your breathing. In both ex-

Craig Beck

amples, you focus on what's inside you rather than the outside. What is the inner body? Well, I guess you could say it is energy inside of your body. How your body feels from the inside.

A practical way to do this is to focus on your hand. Put your focus there and feel how the hand feels to you and how the energy is flowing through it.

Nimm die Stimmung auf

4. Pick up the vibe from present people.

If you know someone that is more present than most people, then you can pick his/her vibe of presence (just like you can pick up positivity or enthusiasm from people).

If you don't know someone like that, I recommend listening to audiobooks by Eckhart Tolle, Brian Tracy, Anthony Robbins, Zig Ziglar or any of the other respected personal development authors out there.

Aufgeben

5. Surrender to the emotion that is already there.

It's easy to get stuck in a loop of old memories. You may want to move away from them, but there is a feeling there that brings them back over and over. So you need to decrease the power that feeling has over you. And you don't do it by fighting it. You do it by surrendering to it.

The feeling is a loop within your mind that you are feeding with more energy by resisting it. When you accept the feeling, then you stop feeding it, and it vanishes. Here's how you do it: Say yes to the feeling. Surrender and let it in. Observe the feeling in your mind and body without labeling or judging it. For me, the feeling seems to physically locate itself in the middle of my chest. If you allow it, and observe it for a minute or two, the feeling just vanishes.

6. See things as if for the first time.

This one is pretty similar to focusing on what's right in front of you, mentioned in the beginning. But it can be useful when you have a hard time just observing your surroundings.

That's when you can look at things as if for the first time. Imagine it like someone who has never experienced this before, like a child or someone who has never been here before.

Note: These next two ways are certainly not the best ways to reconnect with the moment, and I'm not really recommending them. They aren't that healthy (especially in the long run). But they work to some degree. It's up to you if you want to try them.

Kneifen

7. A pinch or a punch!

Try punching your leg, or pinching your arm. Or have someone else do it. And focus on that sensation to quickly bring yourself back to the moment.

Don't go crazy. I am not trying to turn you into a masochist or anything. Just give yourself a little nip and then take a few seconds to experience the feeling. It is purely a distraction that pulls you away from the past or future and allows you to center once again in the present moment.

Free Coaching Video

Here are some great tips to deal with cravings
and keep you on the sober path:

https://www.stopdrinkingexpert.com/
how-to-stop-alcohol-cravings/

DEALING WITH
THE KICK

For most people, once they no longer see alcohol as a benefit, they simply don't want to drink anymore, and so they don't. For others, it takes a little time for the information to be absorbed and to stick. A seed of change has been planted, and over the next few weeks, you will observe a lot more of the adverse effects of alcohol than you ever noticed before. You will see friends at parties slurring their words and believing they are genuinely master orators holding court. You will be surprised that they cannot see that they are anesthetized buffoons talking 100% proof gibberish.

You will notice the sexualization of alcohol by the advertising industry. Of course, typically, the term sex refers to beautiful women (and increasingly, handsome men) that are used to lure in a potential drinker despite a tenuous a non-existent link to the brand being advertised.

You will see television commercials for alcohol and see just how devious they are. Watch them with a critical eye and see how they use sex to hook us into their killer product.

It has been said that as human beings, we have a lizard or reptilian brain that responds to certain primal urges. Food is one. Sex and reproduction are another. This underlying, pre-programmed disposition to respond to sexual imagery is so strong; it has been used for over 100 years in advertising. And the industry, while abusing it more and more, would be foolish to ignore the draw of sexual and erotic messaging.

Back in 1885, W. Duke and Sons, a manufacturer of facial soap, included trading cards in the soap's packaging that included erotic images of the day's most famous female stars. The link between soap and sex is slim at best, but the relationship between alcohol and sex is equally as tenuous, and that works just as well.

Does Sex Sell?

Yes, sex sells. It's a fact. Popular men's magazines like Maxim and FHM have experimented often with their covers. Overwhelmingly, when a sexy, semi-naked woman appears on the cover, it outperforms an image of a male star, even if that star is someone men want to read about.

When ads are more sexually provocative, men, in particular, are irresistibly drawn to them. It's simple genetics. Men respond to sexual images. And if your ad creates a sexual situation, it will get the desired response.

When you consider the science and theory behind sexual advertising, you can see how devious and dishonest it is as a way to encourage people to consume an addictive drug. Using sexual images to tug on genetic responses from customers is a pretty underhand way to promote the use of a product that is a poison. The only reasonable excuse for using sex to promote alcohol would be that it did what it claimed to do. If when you drank a specific brand of alcohol, you looked physically more attractive then fair enough. However, when you live a life free of this attractively packaged poison, you will notice how ugly and repulsive people under the effect of this drug actually become.

Here's a challenge we make at the 'Stop Drinking Expert' members website... After you have been alcohol-free for a couple of months, the first time, you kiss or make out with someone who has been drinking report back to the site and anonymously describe the experience. To date, nobody has told us that kissing a drunk person was a more pleasurable experience - indeed often words such as 'stale', 'tainted' and 'disgusting' get used in the description.

Alcohol advertising tries to create positives from the vast array of negatives generated by this drug. The industry knows that alcohol produces a withdrawal symptom that feels similar to stress, and so they make commercials that portray drinking as a form of relaxation.

When a colleague tells you they can't wait to get home, open a bottle of wine and relax, you will see that statement for what it is. You now know this ritual has nothing to do with relaxation, but rather it is a vocalization of the symptoms of an alcohol kick which by the end of the working day is approaching peak intensity.

Observe these lies being told all around you by your friends, family, and colleagues, but do not feel the urge to point out your observations to anyone. Shining a light on things that people have deliberately placed in the dark is a direct attack on someone's ego, and you can expect nothing but a hostile defense in reply.

For two weeks, providing you don't drink again, your alcohol withdrawal symptoms will get weaker every day. Over that period and for a few weeks after, the supplements you are now taking will slowly begin to have a positive effect. They do not work overnight, and they work differently for everyone. Some people report a massive improvement within a week, others only notice the impact after a month, and a lot of people are not aware of anything happening until they stop taking them and realize what the supplements were contributing.

During the kick, you may experience a few strange sensations. It is highly likely you will dream about drinking alcohol; this is not because you want to drink, but rather a reflection of what is top of your priority list at the moment. You are addressing alcohol as a problem in your life, and so your dreams are built around your current focus. This is why, after watching a movie, you can sometimes dream a similar plotline to what you have just seen, but with yourself playing the role of the protagonist.

When I stopped drinking, I would often wake in the morning feeling convinced I had been drinking heavily the night before, sometimes the dreams were so vivid I would check the garbage for alcohol bottles. Don't be afraid or question the significance of these dreams, as with everything else you observe, simply smile and acknowledge them. These dreams are a good sign, they are evidence that you are going through the same series of events that I did, and the result of that is a complete repulsion to the thought of drinking another alcoholic drink.

Another slightly strange thing to expect is dealing with a slight sense of loss when in situations where you would have previously consumed alcohol.

Before I moved to Cyprus, we used to take regular family vacations on the island. Our vacations usually involved a lot of swimming, reading, sunbathing, eating, and of course drinking. There is that unwritten rule that when you are on holiday, you can drink any time of the day. In the past, I would have had my first alcoholic drink by the pool at around 10 am and slowly kept topping up until bedtime.

The first time we took a vacation after I had quit drinking it felt unusual and a little uncomfortable to be pouring out a can of soda where I would typically have grabbed a cold beer from the refrigerator. My ex-wife was still drinking at this point, and that intensified the sensations somewhat. I wasn't jealous of my wife and her glass of wine, I did not want to drink, but something felt wrong.

Later that night we walked into the seafront bar we would go to most evenings. The owner is a Greek Cypriot called Andreas, and he had always made us feel like old friends returning home. He would play jokes with the kids (including pretending to pour vodka into their lemonade, which made them feel all grown up just like mum and dad).

This particular evening, as we walked into the bar, he noticed us immediately. He rushed out from behind his bar to greet us warmly before ushering us to a table overlooking the Mediterranean. We exchanged small talk for a few moments before he waved at the barmaid still working behind the bar. A few moments later, she came over to join us with a tray of drinks.

Andreas proudly demonstrated his amazing memory again. Despite not having seen us for nearly a year, he placed our usual order of drinks on the table in front of us. A cold glass of wine in front of Denise.

"White for Mrs. Beck," he said in a soft Greek accent.

Next, he reached for two almost fluorescent drinks, tall glasses with a concoction of liquids. The drinks were green at the top, orange most of the way down before turning bright red at the bottom.

"Special cocktails for the children, one Vodka and one Bacardi'," he said with a wink at the grown-ups.

My two children giggled at the suggestion, they knew there was nothing in those glasses but fruit juice and syrup, but they liked the idea that someone might overhear the announcement. It made them feel 'part of the grown-ups gang,' such is the social conditioning of the alcohol drug that children feel like they are missing out on something special!

I smiled as Jordan and Aoife slurped enthusiastically at their 'cocktails,' and then the smile dropped from my face as a huge frosted glass of Leon (the local beer) was lowered from the tray and presented to me.

"Yamas," Andreas cheered and started to walk away.

A few seconds passed by, and I wondered what to do. I didn't want to insult Andreas by sending back the drink, but I most certainly didn't want to drink it. Then I considered that I had not put much thought into why we had gone to the bar in the first place. What was I going to drink? Would I get bored?

We used to spend the whole evening there, slowly getting anesthetized together. When nobody was looking I tipped the beer into a plant pot and quickly ordered a soft drink to be sure he wouldn't diligently refill my glass as he usually would.

I admit, in those moments, I felt like I had lost something, and it made me feel sad. This feeling was tinged with confusion because I was also very aware that I didn't want the thing I had lost. You too will experience these moments, maybe at a wedding or social gathering where all the drinks are provided free. Someone will push one into your hand, and for a moment you will feel sad because you don't want to join in and drink it. In those moments, you must remind yourself that the way you think has nothing to do with the alcohol, it is purely a conditioned response.

A completely unrelated incident that happened in Cyprus helped me get used to the new sober me. The car hire company had messed up our reservation, and when we got to the airport collection desk, they didn't have any record of our booking. They were very apologetic and eventually found us a car, but it was an automatic and not a manual drive. I had never driven an automatic before, and I found not using my left foot or the gear stick very unsettling. For the first few days, I drove that car like a complete novice driver; I sat forward in my chair hugging the steering wheel, concentrating intensely on every single maneuver. I felt exceptionally uncomfortable for about three days, and then it became 'automatic,' if you will excuse the pun.

When I got back home to the UK and jumped in my manual car, I again felt uncomfortable and clumsy. This is exactly what happens when you are put in situations where in the past, you would have drunk. It's not the lack of alcohol that is making you feel bad; it's the slightly uncomfortable sensation of not responding as you are automatically conditioned to do.

If I strapped your right arm to your side and made you live your life for a whole year without using that limb, imagine how strange it would feel using your right hand again after a year. This is how you may feel in circumstances where you would have previously had an alcoholic drink. The more you embed the new reality, the easier it gets; so enjoy each one of those uncomfortable moments and see them as another step on the road to a lifetime of happy sobriety.

There are six steps in my approach to problem drinking. However, the actual process of quitting moves through three unique periods. The first phase, we have already talked about and is what I call 'The Kick.' It is a short period where the drug has the capacity to influence the body physically. Once you are a couple of weeks clear of your last drink, then phase one is complete. It's important to note there is no such thing as 'one little drink'. Any amount of alcohol consumed will take you back to phase one, day one. What this means is one glass of champagne at a wedding is not just one glass. That solitary drink will take 14 days to get out of the system.

At Bootcamp, you will hear me talk of the five most dangerous words you will ever think or say: 'just one drink won't hurt.' I will repeat this sentence many times throughout the day. Firstly because it's one of the most important things you will take home from the event and secondly I know that repetition is the mother of learning.

Saying or thinking 'just one drink won't hurt' is the last thing that will happen before you make a very big mistake. That one event can pull you from the wagon, and it may take many months before you regain your direction. I have seen it happen hundreds of times, and the story always starts the same way. So, I encourage you to remember reading this section of the book, and the first time you ever say those words, punch yourself in the face very hard. Something very bad is about the happen.

Phase Two of the process begins at the same time as phase one but becomes the sole focus after 'The Kick' is done and dusted. Once the drug is clear of your system, any cravings to drink are not being created by alcohol but by the psychological programs in your subconscious mind. The same types of programs that made Pavlov's dogs salivate at the sound of a bell. In order to successfully remove these programs from your unconscious mind, we have to use a series of tools that I refer to as 'the four things.'

Thing One:

I warn you in advance that all of these tools will sound so simple that you wonder how effective they can possibly be. Trust me on this; they work, I have seen thousands of people just like you completely transform their lives using them.

As a problem drinker of many years, the chances are good that you are a little confused about what messages your body is sending you. Because alcohol becomes our panacea for all of life's ups and downs, we tend to go straight to it without really thinking. Often we drink alcohol in response to our central nervous system sending out a message for us to address dehydration. In short, we mistake a sensation of thirst for one of a craving for alcohol. For this reason, if you get the urge to consume alcohol, the very first thing I want you to do is to drink a large, cold glass of water. Then ask yourself if you still feel like grabbing a beer.

It's so easy not to do this. Indeed, all of the tools require conscious commitment, and they will feel awkward and clumsy at first. If you live a busy life, always dashing for here to there. Stopping to find a glass, fill it, and slowly drink water may be an inconvenience. However, you should be aware that this is not something you have to do for the rest of your life. Phase Two lasts around twenty-one days, that's all. In that context, it's really no more inconvenient than what happens when the doctor prescribes you a short course of antibiotics.

Thing Two:

How do you know it's time to drink?

Most people have a routine with their drinking. Full-blown alcoholics drink all day long, but problem drinkers like you and me tend to have a set time or trigger. For me, my routine started the moment I got home from work. Before I took off my coat, said hello to my wife and kids, the corkscrew was in my hand, and I was opening the first bottle of wine. I would head straight to my lazy boy armchair and slowly drink myself into a coma in front of the TV. I had done this every evening for many years. So, when I decided to quit drinking, what do you think is the worst thing I could have done whenever I had a craving to drink?

That's right, drop my ass in that big TV chair. As soon as I sit in that chair, it's like Pavlov ringing his bell. My body will be awash with stimuli to consume alcohol. I am making life so much harder and more difficult than it needs to be. Plus, I am giving power to the programs that I want to erode.

The second 'thing' I want you to do in response to a craving is called a pattern interrupt. We have to stop these old programs running to degrade their power. This means you have to do something dramatically different than what you would typically do.

- Do star jumps for ten minutes

- Run around the block
- Go out into the back yard and jump on the kid's trampoline.
- Go to Zumba
- Call your mom

I don't care what it is, just so long as it is dramatically different from your normal reaction. I freely admit that this can cause disruption in your life. Do you think I wanted to run around the block every time I got the urge to drink? Of course not, I had had a tough day at work and what I really wanted to do was sit and watch my TV. However, I was aware that doing so would only make the journey longer and more difficult. We choose to struggle in the short term to make the future better. The mistake is thinking that there is a way to avoid the struggle, the only choice is whether you get it over with now or keep dealing with it in the future.

Every time you use a pattern interrupt like this; it's similar to dragging a nail across the surface of a CD. If you do it often enough, you will get to the point where that CD won't play anymore. Bingo, this is exactly what we are looking to do with the erroneous programs in your subconscious mind.
Thing Three

If the glass of water and the pattern interrupt hasn't removed your cravings for alcohol, the next tool in the box is tapping therapy, sometimes called thought field therapy. When the cravings are so intense that you feel like there is nothing you can do to stop yourself from pouring a drink. I want you to use a technique called Thought Field Therapy or TFT. Again, this is a principle that appears to be so simple you can't imagine it providing any tangible benefit.

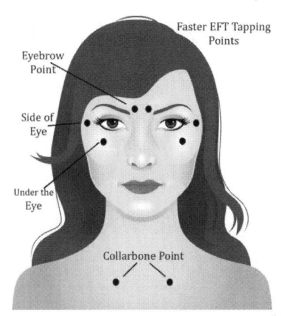

Faster EFT Tapping
Points

Eyebrow
Point

Side of
Eye

Under the
Eye

Collarbone Point

TFT is an acupuncture technique based on the tapping on specific meridian points in the upper body. A renowned Clinical Psychologist called Roger Callahan discovered the principle of TFT in 1980 when he theorized that all negative thought patterns are similar to computer programs that are universally shared by all humans. This is why fear feels the same to me as it does to you, we both run the same program, and so we experience the same physical and mental symptoms of fear accordingly. His system demonstrates that by using unique pressure points in the body, we can turn off the program. It's like a CTRL-ALT-DEL option for negative emotions, anxiety, and most importantly, in our case, cravings.

Next time you need to turn off your cravings for a drink, find a quiet room, anywhere will do. Using your index and middle finger gently start tapping on your cheekbone, directly under the corner of your eye. Tap between ten and twenty times before repeating the process just above your eyebrow. Keep alternating the meridian point and before each change, ask yourself honestly how much you need a drink.

With each series of tapping, give the craving a score out of ten. You may start around the nine or ten levels of 'need,' but you should find that the number slowly reduces with each sequence. Gradually you will find that your desperation moves from 'must have' to 'like to have' before reaching your goal point of 'I can take it or leave it.'

This step is easily dismissed as new age mumbo jumbo, but I don't need you to take my word for it, a quick Google search for evidence of Thought Field Therapy success will show you how successful this technique has been for thousands, if not hundreds of thousands, of other people just like you. There are also plenty of videos showing you how to use this technique on my website.

Thing Four

Daily hypnosis. If you ever see a hypnosis track claiming to be the solution to alcoholism, ignore it. Hypnosis, on its own, is a weak solution to problem drinking. Less than 10% of drinkers will solve their alcohol use disorder using it. However, it is a useful tool in the box. A bit like a spirit level, you may not need it often, but when you do, it's indispensable.

I will cover this in detail in a later chapter, for now, I will offer some advice on the best time of day to listen to one of the downloadable hypnosis mp3 that you will find in the member's area. Quite often people email me and report that they fell asleep during the hypnosis and they wonder if it will 'still work'. Sadly the answer is no and despite all the claims of these snake oil salesmen selling the possibility that you can learn French in your sleep. You need to be awake to receive the positive subliminal messages in these tracks.

To get the maximum possible benefit from the quit drinking hypnosis tracks I have found that this simple rule of thumb helps: If you are a morning person, i.e., you tend to wake up early and be most effective in the first half of the day then I suggest you listen to your daily track at some point before 3 pm. However, if you consider yourself to be a bit of a night owl, then you may find it better to include these tracks into your late afternoon, early evening routine.

That's the four things! Simple right?

Simple but incredibly powerful. If you get a craving for alcohol after Phase One is complete and you diligently apply the four tools above it's highly unlikely you will fall off the wagon. In ten years of helping problem drinkers, I have never once had someone slip up who had done the four things first. Every time someone stumbles and gets in touch with me, I will bet you my house they didn't do what I told them to.

Free Coaching Video

Here are my 5 most powerful tips to building a genuinely happy sober lifestyle:

https://www.stopdrinkingexpert.com/stop-drinking-expert-success/

CHAPTER 13: F.S.Q (FREQUENTLY SLURRED QUESTIONS)

Forgive the quirky play on words, because this section of *Alcohol Lied to Me* may serve a very valuable purpose in your mission to escape the cycle of alcohol addiction. Over the years, I have had many questions emailed to me from problem drinkers (mostly looking for reasons why it would be okay for them to carry on with their drug of choice).

No doubt some of the queries in this ever-expanding section of the book may have popped into your head at some point, so here goes:

Q1. I want to stop drinking, but I work with a pretty tough bunch of guys, and if I didn't drink with them, I wouldn't hear the end of it. Should I just cut down rather than stop drinking?

A1. I can empathize with your situation because we live in a bizarre world where heavy drinking has somehow become associated with being a 'real man.' Back when I was a drinker, I had quite a reputation for being able to 'hold my drink.' As we now know, this tolerance for alcohol should be seen as the first symptom of a serious problem with an addictive drug and not the positive trait that social males so often dictate that it is. I stopped drinking in the winter, November. In the past, I would have postponed this attempt to January because you can't go through a Christmas season without drinking, can you? (Yet another funny lie we have been force-fed.)

When I woke up and realized that it is the rest of the world that is wrong about alcohol and not me, I just decided I didn't want to drink it anymore, so the month had no relevance to me.

in November

However, as easy as I found it to no longer drink, I still had to attend the traditional Christmas party with all my old drinking buddies.

The evening started in a local pub, and my friend Roy walked up to the bar and ordered himself a pint of strong imported beer. He turned to me and said 'Same?' I shook my head and instead asked for a Diet Coke. A few moments passed without further comment, and then it began:

'A Coke! I am not ordering you a Coke. Have a beer and man up,' Roy exclaimed, absolutely disgusted at the very suggestion.

'It's okay Roy I am fine with a Coke,' I replied.

'What's wrong with you man, have you turned gay or something? ' Roy came back.

Perhaps the most ridiculous statement I have ever heard!

I am not sure of the logic behind assuming a decision to no longer voluntarily ingest a toxic chemical must be the result of a change in sexuality, but sadly, it's a statement thrown at heterosexual men who regain control of alcohol all over the world. Drinking vast quantities of alcohol does not prove you are a tough, red-blooded 'man's man'! It proves you are addicted to a common drug!

These sorts of macho put-downs are ridiculous and laughable, but how do you deal with them?

You tough it out! Eventually, your friends will get used to the new, healthier you. The problem, as we've already discussed, is that your high standards highlight their low standards, and it causes them pain; their ego will not tolerate it. Obviously, the best way for them to remove that nagging pain is also to stop drinking, but because the ego hates all forms of loss, it can't accept that prospect and would much rather you started drinking again as a substitute solution.

These days Roy doesn't even need to ask me what I want to drink; he just goes up to the bar orders himself a pint and a Diet Coke for me. He might mutter some comical insult as he hands it to me, but he has accepted the situation, and so will your friends. Do not bend to their attempts to persuade you back into the mousetrap.

Q2. I have heard that milk thistle protects the liver. Can I continue drinking if I take it?

A2. Milk thistle (Silybum marianum) has been used for more than 2,000 years as an herbal remedy for a variety of ailments, particularly liver, kidney, and gall bladder problems. Several scientific studies suggest that substances in milk thistle (especially a flavonoid called silymarin) protect the liver from toxins, including certain drugs such as acetaminophen (Tylenol), which can cause liver damage in high doses. Silymarin has antioxidant and anti-inflammatory properties, and it may help the liver repair itself by growing new cells.

Although some animal studies demonstrate that milk thistle can be helpful in protecting the liver, results in human studies are mixed.

Milk thistle is often recommended as a treatment for alcoholic hepatitis and alcoholic cirrhosis. But scientific studies show inconclusive results. Most studies show milk thistle improves liver function and increases survival in people with cirrhosis or chronic hepatitis. But problems in the design of the studies (such as small numbers of participants and differences in dosing and duration of milk thistle therapy) make it hard to draw any real conclusions.

Whether milk thistle helps or not is a gamble; you can choose to take if you want. If you are seriously considering continuing to drink and supplementing your diet with milk thistle, then I would suggest you have missed the point of this book. Such an act would imply that there is a benefit to continuing to drink alcohol, and this is, quite frankly, insane!

Alcohol is an attractively packaged poison backed by a devious and misleading multi-billion dollar marketing campaign. The solution you are suggesting is likely to be as effective as the smokers who believed that if they didn't inhale deeply, they wouldn't be at such a high risk of developing lung cancer. Any thoughts about ways that you can carry on drinking are just more evidence that you need to get this poison out of your system once and for all.

Q3. How do I avoid drinking at Christmas, Thanksgiving, and on other social occasions?

A3. Well, let me start by asking you how you manage to avoid injecting heroin at Christmas time?

That might sound like a silly question, but in reality, there are only two differences between alcohol and heroin. First, it is just a case of social acceptability; everyone drinks at Christmas, and so we make the false assumption that it is therefore harmless. Just because everyone is doing it does not make it a safe activity. You only have to go back a few decades to when the same twisted logic was applied to smoking. The social proof of smoking did not prevent millions of people from dying in agony from lung cancer. Alcohol is attractively packaged poison whether one person drinks it or a whole nation consumes it.

The second difference between heroin and alcohol is the kick. All addictive substances will punish you if you try to stop your interaction with them. This is known as 'the kick.' Class A street drugs such as heroin trap their users so successfully because the punishment from stopping using is so severe that it takes great determination and endurance to suffer the kick.

The pain of a heroin kick is beyond anything you can imagine, and addicts must endure days of this agony with the knowledge that the pain would vanish in less than a second if they just took another hit of the drug.

Having said that, if you believe that alcohol has the power to make you feel good, then you should try heroin. Wow, heroin can create the feeling of pure ecstasy, a sensation of pleasure beyond our dreams, or so I am told.

So here is the big question — why don't you long for heroin at Christmas and Thanksgiving? It is far superior to alcohol, after all.

The explanation that we keep coming back to is you do not see any benefit to taking heroin. You would not see it as an enhancement to your life – your thinking about this drug is perfectly logical, as it should be about such a dangerous poison. The problem is that your thinking about alcohol is twisted.

If you are thinking about how you can survive your birthday party without a drink, this is just a clear indicator that your thinking is still distorted. You should be thinking about how good it is going to feel to have your first birthday in years that won't result in a horrific hangover.

As far as Christmas is concerned, alcohol has only been added in relatively recent times because it provides a convenient excuse to consume more of our favorite drug. Whether you are religious or not, consider whether alcohol figures anywhere in the traditional story of the birth of Christ? Of course, it doesn't. The three wise men did not turn up with a crate of beer, a bottle of vodka, and some coffee liqueur. These are the trappings of a society trapped in their relationship with an addictive drug.

Look to the east with other similar festivals such as the Hindu celebration of light, Diwali. Five days of festivities, full of fun, laughter, dancing, and merriment, and yet not a single drop of alcohol will cross anyone's lips!

If people tell you that you can't have a good Christmas without a drink, what they are saying to you is, 'I can't cope without alcohol, not even in an environment that is fun and pleasant already.'

Q4. Do you believe the spiritual aspect of AA is wrong?

A4. Absolutely not. Actually, I think it probably makes a significant impact on those that truly embrace it. The problem is that a lot of people will start running as soon as they get a hint of religion or spirituality. It smacks too much of a cult and allows the ego to instantly come up with a thousand reasons why the process won't work.

While I am not religious, you will quickly be able to gather from a Google search of my other books that I am very spiritual-minded. I face most challenges in my life with a specific spiritual technique called Ho'oponopono. I choose not to refer to it in the book until now for the very reasons stated above.

Ho'oponopono is the ancient Hawaiian spiritual process of acceptance, forgiveness, and gratitude. Rosario Montenegro offers one of the most concise stories of how Dr. Hew Len brought this amazing tradition into modern popular culture around the world.

More than thirty years ago, in Hawaii, at the Hawaii State Hospital, there was a special ward, a clinic for mentally ill criminals. People who had committed extremely serious crimes were assigned there either because they had a very deep mental disorder or because they needed to be checked to see if they were sane enough to stand trial. They had committed murder, rape, kidnapping, or other such crimes. According to a nurse that worked there in those years, the place was so bleak that not even the paint could stick to the walls; everything was decaying, terrifying, repulsive. No day would pass without a patient-inmate attacking another patient or a member of the staff.

The people working there were so frightened that they would walk close to the walls if they saw an inmate coming their way in a corridor, even though they were all shackled all the time. The inmates would never be brought outside to get fresh air because of their relentlessly threatening attitude. The scarcity of staff was a chronic occurrence. Nurses, wardens, and employees would prefer to be on sick-leave most of the time in order not to confront such a depressive and dangerous environment.

One day, a newly appointed clinical psychologist, Dr. Stanley Hew Len, arrived at the ward. The nurses rolled their eyes, bracing themselves for one more guy that was going to bug them with new theories and proposals to fix the horrid situation, who would walk away as soon as things became unpleasant, around a month later, usually. However, this new doctor wouldn't do anything like that. He didn't seem to be doing anything in particular, except just coming in and always being cheerful and smiling, in a very natural, relaxed way. He wasn't even particularly early in arriving every morning. From time to time, he would ask for the files of the inmates.

He never tried to see them personally, though. Apparently, he just sat in an office, looked at their files, and to members of the staff who showed an interest, he would tell them about a weird thing called Ho'oponopono. Little by little, things started to change in the hospital. One day somebody would try again to paint those walls, and they actually stayed painted, making the environment more tolerable. The gardens started being taken care of, some tennis courts were repaired, and some prisoners that up until then would never be allowed to go outside started playing tennis with the staff. Other prisoners would be allowed out of their shackles or would receive less heavy pharmacological drugs. More and more obtained permission to go outside, unshackled, without causing trouble to the hospital's employees.

In the end, the atmosphere changed so much that the staff was not on sick leave any more. More people than were needed would now go to work there. Prisoners gradually started to be released. Dr. Hew Len worked there for close to four years. In the end, there remained only a couple of inmates that were eventually relocated elsewhere, and the clinic for the mentally insane criminals had to close.

Simply put, Ho'oponopono is based on the knowledge that anything that happens to you or that you perceive, the entire world where you live, is your own creation. Thus, it is entirely your responsibility.

· Is your boss a tyrant? It's your responsibility.
· Are your children not good students? It's your responsibility.
· There are wars, and you feel bad because you are a good person, a pacifist? The war is your responsibility.
· Do you see that children around the world are hungry and malnourished, even starving? Their want is your responsibility.

No exceptions. Literally, the world is your world; it is your creation. As Dr. Hew Len points out, didn't you notice that whenever you experience a problem, you are there?

That it's your responsibility doesn't mean it's your fault. It means that you are responsible for healing yourself in order to heal whatever or whoever it is that it appears to you as a problem.

It might sound crazy, or just plain metaphorical, that the world is your creation. But if you look carefully, you will realize that whatever you call the world and perceive as the world is your world. It is the projection of your own mind.

If you go to a party you can see how in the same place, with the same light, the same people, the same food, same drink, same music, and same atmosphere, some will enjoy themselves while others will be bored; some will be overenthusiastic and some depressed; some will be talkative and others will be silent.

The 'out there' for every one of them seems the same, but if one were to connect their brains to machines, immediately it would show how different areas of the brain would come alive, how different each person's perceptions are. So even if they apparently share it, the 'out there' is not the same for them, let alone their inner world, their emotions.

How can you use Ho'oponopono to help with giving up drinking?

Three steps: by recognizing that whatever comes to you is your creation, the outcome of bad memories buried in your mind, by regretting whatever errors of body, speech, and mind caused those bad memories, and by requesting divine Intelligence within yourself to release those memories, to set you free. Then, of course, you say thank you.

There are seminars where they teach you many tricks to help this process, but according to Joe Vitale, Dr. Hew Len himself uses the simplest of the formulas from Ho'oponopono. Whenever a matter arises, and they arise incessantly, addressing the Divine within you, you only have to say: 'I'm sorry, Please forgive me, Thank You, I love Yu.'

If you want to discover more about the origins and evidence of Ho'oponopono, lookout for a book by Joe Vitale called *Zero Limits*. Joe goes into great detail about how this amazing principle that has been passed down the ages literally creates miracles.

Q5. I have stopped drinking, and I am really happy about that, but I dream about alcohol every night. Is this normal, and how do I stop it?

A5. Yes, it is completely normal, and sometimes the dreams will be so vivid and detailed that you will wake up completely convinced that you had been drinking during the night.

I remember when I first stopped, I had a dream where I was knocking back shot after shot of neat whiskey. The dream was so lucid that when I awoke, I emptied every garbage bin in the house to make sure there were no empty bottles there. I think I dreamed about drinking for a week solid before they started to slow down. For the first few months of my sobriety, I would have a drinking dream about once a week, and although now it's only about once a year, they still take me by surprise, and I wake up thinking, 'What the heck was that all about?'.

Why this strange phenomenon happens is up for debate. Personally, I believe that it is a combination of reasons. First, your dreams are a way for your brain to filter and sort the information you have absorbed during the day. Your brain files away important information and discards the junk. When you first stop drinking, you are acutely aware of not having a drink in your hand, and you are constantly reminded of situations where before you would have consumed alcohol. As alcohol is still playing an active role in your life, albeit by its absence, it is still considered worthy of processing by your subconscious mind. As you stop noticing the nonappearance of alcohol in your day-to-day life, it will appear less in your dreams accordingly.

The second reason for alcohol dreams is because of a change in brain chemistry. Back when I was drinking, I would rarely manage to make it past 8.00 pm. I would drink a bottle or two of wine and would stumble upstairs to crash into bed, often even before my children's bedtime. I would blink my bloodshot eyes open ten hours later, but I would feel like I had had only about an hour's sleep. This is because alcohol is a mild anesthetic, and despite what the doctor tells you before an operation, anesthesia does not cause sleep but rather a reversible coma.

When you are under general anesthetic, it is not possible to dream because brain activity is slowed to virtually nothing. Dreams are complex and creative actions of the brain, and the chemical is preventing anything but the basic functions to support life.

None of the self-repair and cell regeneration happens during this time, as the brain cannot coordinate the process. When you awake from a drunken 'sleep,' perhaps less than half the night you weren't sleeping at all but were really in an anesthetic-induced coma.

When you have been drinking heavily for a long period of time, the brain and body get used to having this chemical permanently pumping around the system. Stopping drinking is like driving around for a year with the parking brake on the entire time and then suddenly taking if off. When you stop drinking, suddenly the brain has to get used to operating without the brakes on.

The absence of alcohol in the brain is an unusual and significant event that the subconscious has to get its head around (excuse the pun). So it is understandable that this focus would leak into our dreams. Don't worry; perhaps the single biggest reason human beings are at the top of the food chain is because of our ability to adapt. Within weeks these dreams will slow and fade away.

CHAPTER 14: THE NEXT LEVEL

I always say that alcohol addiction is similar to getting stuck in quicksand. In both cases, we make an inaccurate assessment of the risk and the situation. We tend to only address our drinking when we have already started sinking up to our waist. You will notice that in areas where there is quicksand, warning signs are not in the middle of the danger; they are on the perimeter, long before you get near the danger zone.

The same is true of alcohol. When you first take a sip of alcohol and discover, to your shock, that it tastes vile, this should be an alarm bell that scares us off for life. However, we take a look around and notice that everyone else is drinking and apparently enjoying their alcoholic drink. So we persevere, despite all the evidence suggesting that drinking horrible tasting poison for fun is at best ill-advised.

So, we learn how to tolerate alcohol and, to mix our metaphors, we keep walking towards the center of the quicksand. Then when we realize we are sinking, we start to panic and struggle to control our drinking. We use willpower to force ourselves to drink less of the thing we want most in the world. The truth is that using willpower to escape an alcohol problem is as misguided a plan as kicking and struggling are as an effective way to get out of quicksand.

The harsh reality is the more you panic, the deeper you sink.

The more you try to force yourself to go back to being a 'normal' or 'social' drinker of attractively packaged poison, the more you experience failure. Constantly failing to achieve your goal leads to low mood and stress. This increases the problem because we drinkers have a solution for times when we are a bit down in the dumps - we drink!

It's very hard to get out of quicksand on your own. Really what you need is someone to come along, spot you are in trouble and reach out a hand to help you out. That is exactly what I do for people like you!

Reading this book is a powerful first step because not least, you have taken action on a problem that the vast majority of people refuse to deal with. However, if you are otherwise a successful individual with a lot to lose, then refusing to take that helping hand is a gamble with significant consequences.

Consider what could happen to your career, income, reputation, and loved ones if you don't deal with this problem. How would life look like in five years' time if your drinking just kept getting worse?

Helping people escape the trap of alcoholism is my passion. If you ever attend one of my quit drinking events you will see just how much I throw into this. I live it and I breathe it. Every year I work with a handful of people on a one-to-one basis. I effectively become your sponsor. We talk (video) on a regular basis and I make sure you nail this problem once and for all.

I provide the most effective alcohol cessation solution anywhere today.

- Personal mentor calls with Craig Beck
- Custom scripted & recorded hypnosis
- Complete step-by-step video course
- Secret Facebook group
- Inner-circle upgrade

- Non-judgmental community
- Free entry into any live event
- 75 hours of video & audio coaching
- 90 days of intensive support
- Lifetime access & support

If you are interested, visit the website and reserve your place on my next FREE quit drinking webinar.

www.StopDrinkingExpert.com

CHAPTER 15:
SUBCONSCIOUS
REPROGRAMMING

The final step in the 'Stop Drinking Expert' method is subconscious reprogramming. As we have discussed, all the issues we face in life are our responsibility, as they are manifested directly by us, via the programs that run in our subconscious mind. Most of these sub-routines are beneficial and serve a valuable purpose, such as controlling our body temperature and keeping us breathing at the correct rate. However, along our journey through this life, we pick up the odd, erroneous program that creates unhelpful manifestations. These 'bad programs' make us fat, create low self-esteem, and even get us addicted to harmful substances.

Thankfully we are prevented by nature from lifting the hood on the subconscious mind and tinkering with the engine. Of course, our ego would have us believe that we are master mechanics, fully capable of making perfect adjustments to this most powerful of computers. The subconscious knows better, and the gate is kept firmly closed to the overzealous ego.

Using hypnosis we can bypass the conscious mind and implant positive corrections directly into the subconscious. As this part of the mind cannot judge or question, the implanted commands are run exactly as requested.

I have created helpful hypnosis audios that can support you in changing your subconscious thoughts. Using them is optional, and many have stopped drinking
completely without ever having used one of my hypnosis downloads. However, as with everything else I have told you so far, this was an important element for me, and I want you to use every tool in the box to ensure we get the job done. If you do think these powerful audio tracks would help you, then please stop by my website (www.stopdrinkingexpert.com) for the mp3 download details.

It is important that we fully understand what hypnosis is, or more importantly, what it is not. Hypnosis is not black magic, a party trick, nor a piece of theatre. It is a naturally occurring process of the brain that has unfortunately attracted some seriously bad press over recent years; some might say even O.J. Simpson has had better press than hypnosis! Thankfully, for over 2,000 years it was documented and practiced with a great deal of respect. How bizarre that this long studied and amazing function of the human mind was essentially defamed by a man in a bar trying to convince girls to remove their clothes.

Most reputable hypnotherapists and psychologists consider the traditional stage hypnotist to be a blundering incompetent, dabbling in something they don't truly understand. If they truly did understand the amazing potential of real hypnosis, I would think they would do something more productive with it than try to make a person believe they are a little fluffy duck called Roger!

A common misconception about hypnosis is that it is sleep. Although a hypnotized person appears to be sleeping, they are quite alert. Hypnosis is very difficult to describe, as nobody knows what is going on inside the mind of a subject. What we do know is that while in the trance state, the subject becomes very suggestible. A subject's attention, while they are going into trance, is narrowed down gradually.

Many areas of normal communication are removed one by one. Starting with sight, they are asked to close their eyes and concentrate. Other senses are then removed from the equation; some people even lose the complete feeling of their body. That may sound frightening, but it is accomplished in a slow, pleasant way, rather than suddenly turning off a switch.

You enter a world of hyper-relaxation and hyper-awareness. As you might expect, as you remove certain senses, the remaining ones compensate by becoming more acute. Often people who have been under hypnosis will come around and claim, 'It did not work.' When you inquire why they believe hypnosis did not work, they make statements such as, 'I could hear everything. I could even hear the cars going past the window!' This is all part of the misconception that hypnosis is sleep and that during trance you are unconscious when in fact, you are hyperconscious.

I am telling you about hypnosis not because I want you to take to the stage, but because I want you to understand the amazing power of the subconscious mind. A person in a hypnotic state is highly suggestible. The hypnotist has direct access to the person's subconscious without having to go through the conscious mind. This is how they can convince a six-foot-tall, 250lb man he is a light, gentle ballet dancer and have him pirouetting his way around the stage.

Hypnosis is so natural that you do it dozens of times a day without even realizing it. Have you ever driven home at the end of your working day and arrived home with no memory of the journey? Hypnosis just visited you; your brain was using the opportunity of this familiar and fairly simple task to filter and file information in your brain.

You may notice yourself at work blankly staring at the computer screen in a deep, peaceful daydream. This happens due to the vast amount of information constantly entering your brain. Every few hours your mind must pause a little to filter and file all the information you have received, placing it in the correct storage area of the brain.

For example, let's say in the last hour your brain has learned that the color of the walls in the canteen are yellow. It has also learned that your new manager's name is David. It must ensure the information you will need on an ongoing basis is stored close to hand. Unfortunately, this is at the expense of the canteen walls, and I am sorry to say, if questioned, you may have trouble remembering what color those walls were — but who cares, walls may have ears, but I have noticed they stay pretty dumb when asked for a pay rise!

If you are interested in studying the power of hypnosis to a greater extent, I would suggest you read a book called *Patterns of the Hypnotic Techniques of Milton H. Erickson*, by John Grinder.

In my online stop drinking club, I use hypnosis to further embed the six steps of my stop drinking method. I do this because I know that the conscious mind is a guard dog, the sort of animal the mailman must first distract before he opens the gate and creeps up the path to post the mail through the letterbox. After doing so he sneaks back out, hopefully without being noticed. Throughout this book, I have been directly talking to your guard dog. You can choose to accept what I am saying or dismiss it. During hypnosis you do not have that problem; all suggestions are accepted without judgment because the words are directed to the subconscious.

Don't lie there waiting for something magical to happen; don't expect or demand anything. You will also need to be prepared to catch your ego trying to pull you out of the moment. It's fine when it does. If you find your mind wandering, just notice what has happened, smile, and refocus on the now. Relax and let the music and my words drift over you. There is nothing that you can do wrong. Free yourself of that concern and let go of all expectations.

Part of the fear of giving up drinking is that you might spend the rest of your life with an itch you can't scratch, living in a permanent state of wanting a drink but not being able to touch it. This is not a cure; this is a torturous and constant battle with the ego that you can't possibly expect to win in the long term. Imagine being so at ease with alcohol that you can honestly say you don't want a drink, you don't like the taste of it, and if someone pushed a glass of it into your hand, you would rather go out of your way to find a replacement than taking the slightest sip. This state is possible, I know because I have been through the process I have just described to you, and now I live it every day.

As I close this book, I will share with you one final observation from the point of view of an ex-drinker. Recently I was a guest at a wedding set in a beautiful castle in the northeast of England. Everything was perfect — the groom and his ushers were dressed in smart dark grey suits complete with gloves and top hats. The bride looked stunning in a tight-fitting cream bodice and flowing gown.

As the bride walked down the aisle on the arm of her proud father, you could see that she was trembling with nerves and anticipation. As she recited the lines of the marriage ceremony, her voice quivered, and the gathered audience of family and friends made sympathetic and encouraging eyes at her.

At the end of the service, as friends gathered around the happy couple, I was bemused to watch on as the wedding organizer pushed a massive glass of neat whiskey into the bride's hand as though he was a doctor administering a vital antidote.

'Forget the champagne, love. I think it's time for something a bit stronger,' he said as he encouraged the bride to take a big gulp. The bride smiled and thanked him profusely.

Excuse me! Why, at the happiest moment of your life to date, in the precise moment that you had planned and prepared for over several years, in this moment, where all your dreams come true, why would anyone in their right mind knowingly gulp down an anesthetic that dulls their ability to experience reality? It's like planning a dream vacation, saving up the money to go, traveling thousands of miles to get there, and then as soon as you step off the airplane pulling on a blindfold and sticking your fingers in your ears.

There is no situation where alcohol makes our experience better. These days no matter what life throws at me, from the joyful celebration of a party with friends or the pain and grief that comes with the loss of a loved one, I am grateful that I don't need or want alcohol to further complicate the situation. No matter how bad it gets, I know that alcohol can only make it worse, and that is a truly liberating feeling indeed.

Thank you for reading *Alcohol Lied to Me*. I hope this book is the first step you take in your personal journey to finding your own happy, sober life. If you have any questions or need any further advice, please don't hesitate to get in touch.

Craig Beck

Recommended links
- https://www.CraigBeck.com
- https://www.StopDrinkingExpert.com
- https://www.SoberAndOut.com

Follow Craig Beck on Social Media
- Facebook: https://www.facebook.com/craigbeckbooks
- Twitter: http://twitter.com/CraigBeck

You Don't Have to Do It Alone...

Join the online coaching club that has helped over 100,000 people just like you to get back in control of their drinking.

ONLINE COURSE

www.stopdrinkingexpert.com

Are you sick and tired of feeling sick and tired?

Maybe you are finding that more and more you are turning to alcohol on an evening to 'relax' and cope with life?

Perhaps you are dealing with serious health problems, financial worries and failing relationships. Plus the guilt of not giving the people you love the 'real you' anymore?

I understand how you feel!

First of all, you should know that I was a heavy drinker myself. Alcohol became something that I couldn't control despite how miserable it was making me.

I had an outstanding career, beautiful home and family but one by one alcoholism was destroying them all.

Every day I made excuses about why I 'needed' to drink.

All the time, failing to make the connection that my alcoholism was the reason for the vast majority of my problems.

- My health was going downhill fast
- My marriage was falling apart
- I was missing quality time with my children
- My career was going nowhere fast
- I was descending deeper and deeper into debt
- Depression, worry and unhappiness were my life

My drinking was hurting everyone I loved.

My family was everything to me! I would have defended and protected them with my life.

In contrast here I was, badly hurting them myself!

My nightly drinking had turned me into a fat, selfish zombie. I wasn't interested in anything but drinking.

It made me so selfish! As a result I wouldn't go anywhere or do anything unless I could drink at the same time. All clear signs of addiction but still I refused to accept it.

I am ashamed to admit I was a terrible husband and nowhere near the father I set out to be.

There was no way I was going to AA!

I wanted someone to show me how to stop drinking alcohol, but Alcoholics Anonymous was too depressing, also I had my professional reputation to think about. Consequently, I didn't want to stand up in a room full of strangers and label myself 'an alcoholic'.

Rehab was too expensive and I couldn't risk taking an extended leave from work!

I tried almost everything.

From silly gimmicks, herbal supplements and hypnosis through to prescription medication (recklessly ordered from abroad online). It seemed like nothing made any real difference.

FREE QUIT DRINKING WEBINAR

RESERVE YOUR PLACE NOW

www.StopDrinkingExpert.com

Solution' Has Helped Over 100,000 Drinkers

How to stop drinking without all the usual struggle:

When I gave up trying to force myself to cut back. It was only then I discovered how to deal with my alcoholism in a more logical and simple way.

I changed the meaning of alcohol, it stopped being something a saw as a special treat. As a result it became something I saw as nothing more than 'attractively packaged poison'.

Finally, life suddenly became... peaceful, happy and secure.

I lost weight, slept like a baby, reconnected with my family, regained my career and even more.

It became so easy that the years I had struggled to force myself to cut back seemed silly.

I had tried hundreds of times to moderate my drinking. All the time dreaming of drinking like a 'normal' person.

Creating silly rules for myself:

- I told myself I would only drink beer, never wine (FAILED)
- Then I promised I would only drink on special occasions (FAILED)
- I said I would quit drinking at home and only drink socially (FAILED)
- Yet, In all other areas of my life I was successful.

Nobody outside my close family had any idea I was knocking back two bottles of wine a night, every night.

My friends just thought I could 'handle my drink', like it was something to be proud of!

FREE QUIT DRINKING WEBINAR

RESERVE YOUR PLACE NOW

www.StopDrinkingExpert.com

Then I Had A Lightbulb Moment!

Everyone claims that quitting drinking is difficult, miserable and painful right?

The reason is because drinkers the world over are using the same broken 'solution' over and over and expecting the outcome to change.

Trying to force yourself to moderate your drinking has a 95% chance of failure.

So why then does EVERY traditional way of dealing with alcohol addiction still uses this as the 'go to solution'?

Perhaps willpower does not work?

Twelve-step programs tell you that you are broken and always will be

Consequently, you must spend the rest of your life forcing yourself to stay away from the thing you want the most!

Likewise, rehab costs tens of thousands of dollars to do exactly the same thing.

Using prescription medication to deal with any addiction still requires willpower in order to keep taking the tablets.

Plus they come with side-effects worse than a hangover!

Absolutely no judgment or embarrassment - Deal with this entirely in the privacy of your own home.

If it wasn't killing over three million people every year (according to World Health Organization figures) it might even be funny.

But for those of us trapped in the loop, it's not funny. It's a miserable experience.

Therefore, these days I devote my time to showing people how to stop drinking alcohol in a rather more simple way. No embarrassing group meetings, no expensive rehab, no dangerous medications and absolutely zero ineffective willpower.

Your health is going to get dramatically better

Within 3 months of quitting drinking my high blood pressure vanished. More than that, it return to perfectly normal levels, despite being elevated for over a decade.

My sleep apnea cleared up and the scary pain in my side went away and never came back. Therefore, proving to me once and for all that it was being caused by my drinking all along.

Who knows what would have happened if I had carried on drinking.

I lost 57lbs of body fat without any real effort. It turns out there is a lot of calories in all that alcohol I was knocking back.

But my story is not unique. You are about to find out for yourself the significant health benefits of kicking the attractively packaged poison out of your life:

1. Better quality sleep.
2. More energy.
3. Clarity and less brain fog.
4. Clearer skin.
5. Increased mental focus.
6. Effortless weight loss.
7. Improved blood pressure.
8. Reduced risk of cancer.
9. Better immune system.
10. Improved memory function.

Your relationships will get so much better

If you are a problem drinker your relationships are under an unbearable amount of pressure.

The hard truth is, drinkers are focused on when they can have their next drink. As a result they don't spend a lot of time considering how they can be a loving, caring and passionate husband or wife.

When you learn how to stop drinking alcohol using my method, so many good things happen to your relationships:

1. No more drunken arguments and saying things you will regret.
2. More quality time together.
3. Never choosing alcohol over your partner again.

4. Sexual dysfunction and impotence can improve.
5. More passionate and enjoyable sex where you are both 100% present.
6. Stop giving your partner the 'lazy zombie' version of the person they met.
7. Be the loving, attentive parent that you set out to be.
8. Rediscover the authentic you.

Plus: The average member saves thousands... every year

The average member saves over $6000 per year. But alcohol is stealing so much more than the financial cost!

When you're sober, you naturally operate at your maximum capacity. You're lucid, focused, and you wake up feeling like a million bucks every day (this benefit cannot be overstated).

When I was drinking, my effectiveness on any given day might have been around 80%.

Now, I feel like I'm constantly operating at 98% or more. What's incredible is that this improvement has had an exponential impact on the tangible success I've achieved.

Get back in control of your life easily with this course

I always dreamed of escaping the rat race and being my own boss. For over a decade my drinking problem prevented me from even getting started.

As soon as I discovered how to stop drinking alcohol for good, my life started to change in the most amazing ways.

I quit drinking and then I quit my miserable 9 to 5 job. Today, I never go to 'the office', likewise, I am never stuck in the dreaded commute and I don't have a boss to answer to.

Thousands of people just like you have done exactly the same thing with my help...

Just as soon as they kick this life limiting poison out of their lives for good.

Decide now & be the next to quit drinking without any of the usual hard work or struggle.

FREE QUIT DRINKING WEBINAR

RESERVE YOUR PLACE NOW

www.StopDrinkingExpert.com

Sign up for my next free quit drinking webinar and I will personally take you through the easy, step by step process:

1. How to escape problem drinking safely, quickly & easily
2. Dealing with your drinking friends and family
3. Relaxing without a drink
4. Dealing with stress and anxiety
5. Destroy all cravings in 3 easy moves
6. Sleep better and rest better
7. How to vacation & celebrate without alcohol (and have a great time)
8. Retaking control of life and going after your dreams.

QUIT DRINKING BOOTCAMP

I understand where you currently are. I was a heavy drinker myself (for nearly two decades). Alcohol became something that I couldn't control despite how miserable it was making me.

I had a great job, beautiful home and family but... one by one alcoholism stole them all from me. Every day I made excuses about why I 'needed' to drink. All the time, I failed to make the connection that my alcohol use was the reason for the vast majority of my problems.

AA was too depressing, and I didn't want to label myself as an alcoholic. Rehab was too expensive for my joyless and broke self. **Finally,** I realized willpower was not the answer to control my alcohol intake.

For nearly a decade I'd been fighting a losing battle!

When I eventually landed on a more logical method **of controlling my cravings for alcohol** without willpower or withdrawal. Life suddenly became peaceful and secure. I lost weight, slept like a baby, reconnected with my family, and regained my career.

Now I take this knowledge around the world with my highly respected

Quit Drinking Bootcamp.

What to expect from Quit Drinking Bootcamp

- The Live quit drinking events are always small, friendly & non-judgmental. There will be no more than 20 people attending. Everyone in the room is in the same situation.
- You will not have to stand up (AA style) and label yourself an alcoholic (or anything at all). You can be as actively or passively involved as you want.
- The event is 100% private, confidential, and discreet. There will be no mention of alcohol on your card statement or anywhere at the venue.
- Dress comfortably, grab a coffee, and turn up at least ten minutes before the start time. Craig will take it from there. Take notes if you want, but it's not essential.
- The days run roughly 10 am to 4.30pm. There will be several comfort breaks and a chance to take a breather and grab some lunch.
- There is nothing further to buy, no up-selling & no need to attend any additional seminars. The event works in one day by deconstructing the foundations of why you turn to alcohol.
- There is no pressure to do anything. You don't even have to commit to stop drinking altogether - that will always be your choice.
- Come along sober, optimistic, and with an open mind. Follow the steps, and you will be able to quit drinking easily,

painlessly, and without willpower.

For dates and ticket information visit www.StopDrinkingExpert.com/ quit-drinking-bootcamp/

Printed in Germany
by Amazon Distribution
GmbH, Leipzig

19700580R00113